I0006756

MCDST Exam Review
70-271 & 70-272

Neil R.Tucker

©2006 by Neil R. Tucker
All rights reserved.

ISBN: 978-1-4303-0491-3

Published in the United States of America.

Introduction

This exam review guide is designed to help you assess your preparedness for the MCDST exams. Each chapter maps to a specific objective you must understand before taking the test. A preparation guide and list of exam objectives can be found in the appendix.

If you also want to try an online simulation exam, try taking one of these tests at www.testgurus.net. You will also have access to additional and updated questions from the web-site. The email questions also allow you to pace your study and review information daily.

The best way to use the guide is to use it to determine the objectives in which you are weakest. By focusing your study in these areas, you will use your time more efficiently in preparing for your test. Check out the www.testgurus.net web-site for additional exam preparation help and materials.

Table of Contents

Section A: Exam 70-271
Chapter 1: Installing a Windows Desktop Operating System

1. What configuration file contains information about the boot order of operating systems on a desktop?

- ☐ A. boot.ini
- ☐ B. ntldr
- ☐ C. bootsect.dos
- ☐ D. autoexec.bat

2. What is the name of the setup program used to install Windows XP on a system that had no previous operating system?

- ☐ A. winnt32.exe
- ☐ B. setup.exe
- ☐ C. install.exe
- ☐ D. winnt.exe

3. What command would you use to upgrade Windows 2000 to XP if you are doing a manual installation?

- ☐ A. winnt.exe
- ☐ B. winnt32.exe
- ☐ C. upgrade.exe
- ☐ D. setup.exe

4. What parameter is used to do an unattended install on a desktop with no previous operating system?

☐ A. winnt.exe /u
☐ B. winnt.exe /unattend
☐ C. winnt32.exe /u
☐ D. winnt32.exe /unattend

5. When doing an unattended install with the /s parameter what information are you giving?

☐ A. The name of the answer file
☐ B. The name of the uniqueness file
☐ C. The path to the setup files
☐ D. The path to the service pack upgrade files

6. After doing an installation you decide to install the latest service pack. What must you do to ensure that all previous updates will also be included?

☐ A. Install the earlier service packs after the latest one is installed
☐ B. The earlier service packs must be installed first and in the correct order
☐ C. Install the latest service pack and then install the earlier ones when you are prompted to do so
☐ D. Nothing.

7. You will be performing unattended setups on twelve computers using a preconfigured answer file. What other file is needed for this procedure to work?

☐ A. udf
☐ B. source
☐ C. extended
☐ D. extension

Installing a Windows Desktop Operating System

8. What configuration file will contain information about all the operating systems configured on a multi-boot system?

☐ A. config.sys
☐ B. ntldr
☐ C. autoexec.bat
☐ D. boot.ini

9. What is the minimum RAM configuration for a computer that will be upgraded to Windows XP?

☐ A. 32MB
☐ B. 64MB
☐ C. 128MB
☐ D. 256MB

10. You install windows XP on a computer that designates the C: drive as the active partition. The operating system files were installed at D:WINDOWS. The only drive configured as NTFS is the E: drive. The largest partition is 20 GB and designated as F:. Which of these drives is the system partition?

☐ A. C
☐ B. D
☐ C. E
☐ D. F

11. Which of the following command can you use to create a partition?

☐ A. Format
☐ B. Convert
☐ C. Compress
☐ D. Fdisk

12. How can you create Windows XP boot disk to start the setup process for a computer?

☐ A. Use the /bootdsk parameter during setup
☐ B. Download them from the Microsoft Web-Site
☐ C. Use the sys.com command on the setup CD to create them
☐ D. Use the makeboot command

13. Which of the following commands would work best for backing up user profile information to be used on another system?

☐ A. scanstate
☐ B. loadstate
☐ C. gpupdate
☐ D. ntbackup

14. You have upgraded desktops running Windows 95, Windows NT 4.0 and Windows 2000 to Windows XP. Which of these platforms can be restored to their previous confiiguration by uninstalling Windows XP?

☐ A. None of them
☐ B. Windows 95
☐ C. Windows NT 4.0
☐ D. Windows 2000

15. You are configuring a multi-boot system that will be running Windows 98; Windows NT 4.0; Windows 2000 and XP for testing purposes. What is the minimum number of partitions necessary to support this configuration?

☐ A. One
☐ B. Two
☐ C. Three
☐ D. Four

16. In a boot.ini file what does a configuration where multi(1) is stated mean?

☐ A. The operating system is on the first hard-drive
☐ B. The operating system is on the second hard-drive
☐ C. The operating system is on a drive controlled by the first disk controller
☐ D. The operating system is on a drive controlled by the second disk controller

17. On a system that uses only IDE controllers what does the disk(1) parameter mean in a boot.ini file?

☐ A. Nothing
☐ B. You are working with the first hard-disk
☐ C. You are working with the second hard-disk
☐ D. You are working with the second disk controller

18. Your computer runs three operating systems with Windows 2000 being the default one loaded at boot time. What tool or file can you use to make Windows XP the default operating system?

☐ A. BIOS
☐ B. ntldr
☐ C. boot.ini
☐ D. system.ini

19. You want to perform a CD based install of Windows XP on a system that does not have a bootable CD-ROM. Which of the following solutions would solve this problem?

☐ A. Use a Windows 98 boot disk to gain access to the CD-ROM and start the install from there.
☐ B. Change the CD-ROM status to bootable in the BIOS
☐ C. Change the order of boot devices in the BIOS
☐ D. Connect the CD-ROM to the first disk controller

20. You connect a computer to your network using a MS-DOS 6.22
network boot disk to start the install of Windows XP. It is not able to
see the C: drive however which is formatted as a 2 Gigabyte FAT32
partition. Why can the boot disk not see the C: drive?

☐ A. The partition size is too large to be recognized by DOS
☐ B. The partition was created as a primary partition
☐ C. The partition was created as an extended partition
☐ D. DOS does not recognize FAT32 partitions

21. You have an 8 gigabyte partition on a system where you will
install Windows XP. Which of the following file systems can you use
to start the unattended install?

☐ A. FAT
☐ B. FAT32
☐ C. NTFS
☐ D. HPFS

22. What is the function of smartdrv.exe on a MS-DOS startup disk?

☐ A. It analyzes the status of your hard-drive
☐ B. It is used to create or delete new partitions
☐ C. It improves the speed of file copy operations
☐ D. It is used to create or delete new file systems

23. Which log file generated by the Windows XP setup process will
give information about errors detected during install?

☐ A. setuplog.txt
☐ B. setuperr.log
☐ C. error.log
☐ D. setup.txt

24. Which of the following files will record tasks that were performed during the Windows XP setup process?

☐ A. setuplog.txt
☐ B. setup.txt
☐ C. install.txt
☐ D. install.ini

25. You are doing an unattended setup for twenty (20) new desktops on your network. Their configuration will be identical. Which configuration file will most likely contain the display settings for all the computers?

☐ A. unattend.txt
☐ B. unattend.udf
☐ C. unattend.bat
☐ D. setup.txt

26. You will be performing an unattended setup for some new machines on your network. Which configuration file will contain the computer names for these machines?

☐ A. unattend.txt
☐ B. unattend.udf
☐ C. setup.txt
☐ D. autoexec.bat

27. You will be configuring a dual boot install on your system thats running Windows 98 on the C: drive. The Windows XP install must have a secure file system. Which of the following solutions will accomplish this?

☐ A. Convert the C: drive to NTFS when Windows XP is installed on it

☐ B. Create an additional partition and use FAT32 for the XP install on it

☐ C. Convert the C: drive to FAT32 when Windows XP is installed on it

☐ D. Create an additional partition and use NTFS for the XP install on it

28. What tool is used to strip out unique information from a computer before a network image is made of the Operating System?

☐ A. Sysprep
☐ B. Fdisk
☐ C. Winnt32
☐ D. Scanstate

29. You want to permanently install the Recovery Console on a desktop used for testing. Which of the following commands will do this?

☐ A. It cannot be done.
☐ B. winnt.exe /cmdcons
☐ C. winnt32.exe /cmdcons
☐ D. console.exe

30. You are using System Restore to replace corrupted registry files on a computer. A typical install of Windows XP was done on the system. What location should the files be copied to?

☐ A. c:\windows
☐ B. c:windows\system32\config
☐ C. c:\windows\system\config
☐ D. c:\windows\system32

Section A: Exam 70-271
Chapter 2: Managing and Troubleshooting Access to Resources

31. If a user belongs to two groups that have access to a folder how is the users effective permissions calculated?

☐ A. He will get the permissions of the least restrictive group
☐ B. He will get the permissions of the more restrictive group
☐ C. He will get the combined permissions of both groups
☐ D. He will get the permissions of the group with the higher priority

32. What command can you use to change a FAT32 partition to NTFS without the loss of any files?

☐ A. convert
☐ B. change
☐ C. upgrade
☐ D. Disk Management

33. What can the NTFS modify permission do that the write permission cannot?

☐ A. Change a files content
☐ B. Change a files name
☐ C. Delete a file
☐ D. Change a files attributes

34. In what situation are share permissions used instead of NTFS for network users?

☐ A. When they are less restrictive
☐ B. When they are more restrictive
☐ C. Never
☐ D. When the user is not an Administrator or Power User

35. In what situation will you not be able to assign unique permissions for different groups of users to a share?

☐ A. If you are using Simple File Sharing
☐ B. If the share is not on an NTFS folder
☐ C. If you did not use Administrator priveleges to create the share
☐ D. If the Read-Only attribute is enabled on the folder being shared

36. Which of the following would prevent you from encrypting a file on your hard-drive?

☐ A. You are not logged in as an Administrator or Power User
☐ B. The file system is FAT32
☐ C. The file is in a folder that is being shared
☐ D. You are not the owner of the document

37. Which of the following commands will share the folder C:\TEMP with the name TEMP$?

☐ A. net share c:\temp=temp
☐ B. new share c:\temp=temp
☐ C. new share temp=c:\temp
☐ D. net share temp=c:\temp

38. A user has just been added to a group to give him access to a shared resource. What must he do to take advantage of his new permissions?

☐ A. Nothing
☐ B. Run the gpupdate command
☐ C. Logout and login again
☐ D. Reboot one of the Domain Controllers

39. You are trying to compress some files on your C: drive but are unable to do so. Which of the following could be the cause?

☐ A. Your C: drive is the system partition and files on this drive cannot be compressed
☐ B. The file system is FAT32
☐ C. You have disabled off-line files
☐ D. The file is in the root folder

40. Which of the following features cannot be used at the same time as file encryption?

☐ A. File Compression
☐ B. File Permissions
☐ C. Off-line Files
☐ D. Folder Sharing

41. You are unable to modify the permissions on a folder for a particular group even though you can do this for other groups. What is one possible explanation for this?

☐ A. The folder is on a FAT32 partition
☐ B. The folder is on a network share
☐ C. The permissions were inherited
☐ D. You do not have Administrator Priveleges on the folder

42. You are trying to share a folder but are unable to do so. Which of the following is a plausible reason for this?

☐ A. You do not have Full Control permissions on the folder
☐ B. The file system is FAT32
☐ C. The file system if NTFS 4.0
☐ D. The folder is on a network connected drive

43. You are assigning permissions to a network share that is on an NTFS drive. How should you assign the permissions?

☐ A. On the share and on NTFS
☐ B. On the Share only
☐ C. On NTFS only
☐ D. In Active Directory

44. What command-line tool is used to compress files?

☐ A. compact
☐ B. compress
☐ C. encrypt
☐ D. zip

45. What are the effective permissions of a network user who has Full Control on a share but has been denied permissions on NTFS?

☐ A. He will have no access
☐ B. He will have Full Acess
☐ C. His permissions will depend on his Primary Group
☐ D. His permissions will depend on the Active Directory priority of Shares vs. NTFS

46. What permissions will a user have to a local folder if his NTFS permissions give him Full Control but its Share permissions deny him access?

☐ A. Full Control
☐ B. No Access
☐ C. It depends on the priority setting for NTFS vs. Shares in the local policies
☐ D. Read Access

47. A user is unable to browse for a particular share on another Windows XP system although the others are accessible. The computer is named COMPUTER23 and the share is named FRIDAY$. What could be causing this problem?

☐ A. The computer has NETBIOS turned off
☐ B. The computer name is invalid for NETBIOS
☐ C. The share is hidden because of the $ sign
☐ D. FRIDAY is a special name and cannot be used for a share

48. Which of the following tools can you use to enable Offline Files on your computer?

☐ A. Device Manager
☐ B. Windows Explorer
☐ C. Hardware Wizard
☐ D. Hardware Profile

49. A user tries to install a local printer but is unable to do so because of his limited privileges. Which of the following local groups will give the user permissions to do this?

☐ A. Guests
☐ B. Users
☐ C. Backup Operators
☐ D. Power Users

50. What UNC path will you use to connect to a printer named HP_Laser_Jet if it has a share name of HPLASERJ on a server named PRINTSERVER1?

☐ A. \\PRINTSERVER1\HPLASERJ
☐ B. \\HP_Laser_Jet\PRINTSERVER1
☐ C. \\PRINTSERVER1\HP_Laser_Jet
☐ D. \\HP_Laser_Jet\HPLASERJ

51. Which of the following is a requirement for setting up a printer pool?

☐ A. The share name must be hidden on the network
☐ B. All the print devices must be able to use the same driver
☐ C. The printers must point to the same print device
☐ D. The printers must point to the same port

52. You try to enable offline files on your home computer running Windows XP Home Edition but cannot do so. Why is this the case?

☐ A. It is not joined to a domain
☐ B. There is no network card or it has been disabled
☐ C. You are not running at least service pack 1
☐ D. This version of XP does not support offline files

53. A users My Documents folders has been redirected to a network share. He now asks you to configure his work laptop to automatically keep a copy of the files he works with so he can work from home. What feature configuration on his laptop would best accomplish this?

☐ A. Disable Folder Redirection
☐ B. Enable EFS
☐ C. Enable the Index Service
☐ D. Enable offline files

54. Which of the following UNC paths points to a hidden share?

☐ A. \\SERVER1\$SHARE0
☐ B. \\SERVER1\SHARE0$
☐ C. \\SERVER1\SHARE0#
☐ D. \\SERVER1\#SHARE0

Section A: Exam 70-271
Chapter 3: Configuring and Troubleshooting Hardware Devices and Drivers

55. How many partitions can you create on a hard-drive if you are running the Windows XP operating system?

☐ A. Two
☐ B. Four
☐ C. Eight
☐ D. Sixteen

56. You must create six separate drives on a new hard-drive. Which of the following will allow you to accomplish this?

☐ A. Create an extended partition
☐ B. Create a logical partition
☐ C. Create a primary partition
☐ D. Create a mounted partition

57. What is the maximum number of extended partitions that can be created on a hard-drive?

☐ A. One
☐ B. Two
☐ C. Four
☐ D. Eight

58. Which of the following is NOT a requirement for mounting a partition to a drive?

☐ A. The drive you are mounting to must be NTFS
☐ B. The drive you are mounting to must have at least 1 metabyte of drive space free
☐ C. The drive must have an empty folder
☐ D. The drive you are mounting cannot already have a drive letter assigned to it

59. Which of the following configuration options will do a complete shutdown of your computer?

☐ A. Hibernate
☐ B. Standby
☐ C. Offline Files
☐ D. Shadow Copies

60. What system component would you use to reconfigure your computer to boot to the CD-ROM media before using the hard-drive on startup?

☐ A. Cannot be done.
☐ B. BIOS
☐ C. System Properties
☐ D. config.sys

61. Which of the following configurations would most likely benefit from the use of a hardware profile?

☐ A. A computer with a hot swapable drive
☐ B. A network card that can switch between 10 and 100 megabits
☐ C. A laptop with a docking station
☐ D. A desktop that switches between two Monitors

62. You want to configure your system to use a multi-monitor configuration by means of three video cards. What is one requirement for these video cards?

☐ A. They must be PCI or AGP cards
☐ B. They must all use the same driver
☐ C. They must be configured before the operating system install process
☐ D. They must be from the same manufacturer

63. You are using a multi-monitor configuration on your system. Which of the following statements is not true about configuring such a setup?

☐ A. The video cards can be either PCI or AGP
☐ B. You can use up to ten video cards
☐ C. The monitors must use the same video resolution
☐ D. You cannot use an ISA video card

64. At what stage in the boot process will you be allowed to choose a hardware profile?

☐ A. Before the information in CMOS is loaded
☐ B. After the Services are loaded
☐ C. After the Operating System is chosen in the boot loader
☐ D. After the drivers are loaded

65. After installing a new driver for one of your SCSI controllers it no longer works properly. What is the easiest way to get back the older configuration without losing any other system changes?

☐ A. Last Known Good Configuration
☐ B. Driver Roll Back
☐ C. System Restore from yesterday
☐ D. ASR Backup

66. Some users on your network have had trouble with software drivers that they install on their systems that cause system crashes. How can you best control this problem without affecting their other privileges?

☐ A. Configure Driver Signing
☐ B. Remove users from the local Administrators group on their system
☐ C. Use Task Manager to end frozen applications
☐ D. Prevent users from changing desktop icons

67. Which of the following tools can you use to create a list of all drivers installed on your system?

☐ A. driverlist
☐ B. driverquery
☐ C. driververif
☐ D. sigdriver

68. You need to reconfigure the default I/O settings for one of the plug-and-play devices on your computer. Where can this be done?

☐ A. system.ini
☐ B. boot.ini
☐ C. Hardware Profile
☐ D. Device Manager

69. Which command-line tool can you use to assign a new driver letter to a partition?

☐ A. diskpart
☐ B. format
☐ C. fdisk
☐ D. convert

70. A user has asked you to configure the Hibernation and Standby settings for their new laptop. Which of the following statements is true concerning this configuration?

☐ A. Standby Mode cannot be configured unless Hibernation is configured first
☐ B. Hibernation cannot be configured unless Standby is configured first
☐ C. Hibernation will do a complete shutdown of the system
☐ D. Standby will copy the information in memory to your hard-drive

71. After installing an incorrect video driver you decide to boot with a generic VGA driver to fix the problem. Which of the following will accomplish this?

☐ A. Safe Mode
☐ B. VGA Mode
☐ C. Last Known Good Configuration
☐ D. Debug Mode

72. A user is complaining that the user before changed the video settings and now the items on his screen are too small to read. What should he do to fix this problem?

☐ A. Decrease the font DPI
☐ B. Decrease the screen resolution
☐ C. Increase the screen resolution
☐ D. Delete his user profile and logon with a new one

73. You are having some trouble getting a new USB device to be recognized by your computer. It is connected to a USB hub and all the five other devices on it are working. What is one possible cause of this problem?

☐ A. Bad USB Hub
☐ B. The cable connecting the USB hub to your computer is bad
☐ C. The cable connecting the new device to the USB hub is bad
☐ D. The USB controller is disabled in the BIOS

74. You are trying to configure hibernation on your Windows 2000 Professional desktop computer but are unable to do so. What could be the cause of this problem?

☐ A. ACPI support was not installed
☐ B. You do not have a Network bootable NIC card
☐ C. Hibernation support does not exist on Windows 2000 systems
☐ D. Hibernation cannot be configured on desktops

75. You need your laptop to automatically power down the monitor and hard-drive after 30 minutes of inactivity. Which of the following options will allow you to do this?

☐ A. Hibernation
☐ B. Power Schemes
☐ C. Screen Saver
☐ D. ACPI Configuration

76. After connecting a USB drive to your system what else must you do to access its resources?

☐ A. Use the Disk Management tool to run Rescan and find the drive
☐ B. Use the Disk Management tool to run Refresh and find the drive
☐ C. Nothing
☐ D. Use the diskpart command-line utility to run Rescan and find the drive

77. What is one advantage that IEEE 1394 devices have over USB devices?

☐ A. Speed
☐ B. Plug and Play Technology
☐ C. Support for more devices
☐ D. It uses a wireless standard

Section A: Exam 70-271
Chapter 4: Configuring and Troubleshooting the Desktop and User Environments

78. Which of the following commands can you use to create a user account?

☐ A. new user
☐ B. net user
☐ C. create user
☐ D. add user

79. What must a user do to ensure that his profile is not used by another user who logs onto his machine?

☐ A. Change the computer to use Fast User Switching
☐ B. Change the computer to not use Fast User Switching
☐ C. Change his configuration to use a roaming profile
☐ D. Nothing

80. A legally blind user needs a way to increase the size of different areas on his screen while working. Which of the following options would help in this situation?

☐ A. On-Screen Keyboard
☐ B. Magnifier
☐ C. Narrator
☐ D. Multiplier

81. A legally blind user wants a way to identify different options as he works in applications on his desktop. Which of the following options would help?
☐ A. On-Screen Keyboard
☐ B. Task Manager
☐ C. Screen Sizer
☐ D. Narrator

82. What database is used to authenticate local user accounts?

☐ A. same
☐ B. Active Directory
☐ C. ntds.dit
☐ D. wins.mdb

83. How can a user open an application with different credentials from the one he is already logged in with without changing his existing login status?

☐ A. Fast User Switching
☐ B. Secondary Logon
☐ C. It cannot be done
☐ D. Change the application to Windows 98 compatibility mode

84. A user on your local network is unable contact a domain controller for authentication purposes during logon. Which of the following services if improperly configured could be causing this problem?

☐ A. RAS
☐ B. WINS
☐ C. IIS
☐ D. DNS

85. Your manager has decided to use multi-factor authentication to ensure more secure logons. Which of the following describes a multi-factor authentication method available on Windows XP?

☐ A. Dial-Up
☐ B. VPN
☐ C. Smart Card
☐ D. Username and Passwords

86. A user running Windows 2000 wants to create a disk that allows him to reset his password if he forgets it. How can this be done?

☐ A. Create a backup of his profile
☐ B. Use the Recovery Console
☐ C. Create a Password Reset Disk
☐ D. It cannot be done.

87. Which of the following tools can you use to monitor Processor performance and close applications that eat up too much of your system resources?

☐ A. Task Manager
☐ B. System Monitor
☐ C. Network Monitor
☐ D. Performance Logs and Alerts

88. One of the users on your network wants to enable Fast User Switching on her desktop but is unable to do so. What is one possible cause of this problem?

☐ A. The computer is a member of a Workgroup
☐ B. The computer is running Windows 2000
☐ C. She does not have Domain Admin Privileges
☐ D. The computer is not a laptop

89. A user is unable to change his configuration to use Fast User Switching and asks for your help. Which of the following might be causing this?

☐ A. This computer is a member of a domain
☐ B. The system was upgraded from Windows 2000
☐ C. The screen resolution is too low
☐ D. He is using a local user account

90. Which of the following tools is used to create a domain user account?

☐ A. Computer Management
☐ B. Windows Explorer
☐ C. Active Directory Users and Computers
☐ D. Local Security Policy

91. Which of the following tools can you use to reset the password of a local user account?

☐ A. System Monitor
☐ B. Local Security Policy
☐ C. Active Directory Users and Computers
☐ D. Computer Management

92. A user wants to have his desktop configuration duplicated on each new computer he logs into so he does not have to reconfigure it each time. What is the best way for you to help him?

☐ A. Configure a mandatory profile for him
☐ B. Configure a roaming profile for him
☐ C. Copy his profile to each of the computers he uses
☐ D. Copy his profile to the Default User Profile

93. A user wants to reconfigure his local user account to have a roaming profile. How can he do this?

☐ A. Use the Computer Management Tool to reconfigure his account settings
☐ B. Use Active Directory Users and Computers to reconfigure his account settings
☐ C. Delete his account and recreate it with a roaming profile
☐ D. It cannot be done.

94. You need to create a profile for a group of users with desktop settings that cannot be permanently changed by them. What type of profile will allow you to do this?

☐ A. Roaming
☐ B. Default
☐ C. Local
☐ D. Mandatory

95. When a user first logs onto a computer from where does his initial profile settings come?

☐ A. Default User Profile
☐ B. Administrator Profile
☐ C. Local Profile
☐ D. General Profile

96. Which taskbar toolbar allows you to directly specify web-sites you want to browse?

☐ A. Address
☐ B. Quick Launch
☐ C. Links
☐ D. Desktop

97. Which of the following commands will create a group named GROUP1 on your Windows XP desktop?

☐ A. net group /add group1
☐ B. net localgroup /add group1
☐ C. net group group1
☐ D. net localgroup group1

98. In what order are Group Policy settings applied in a domain environment?

☐ A. Local Computer > Domain > OU > Site
☐ B. Domain > Local Computer > OU > Site
☐ C. Local Computer > Site > Domain > OU
☐ D. Site > Local Computer > Domain > OU

99. How does Active Directory apply Group Policy settings when they conflict with each other?

☐ A. The last policy setting to be applied will prevail
☐ B. The first policy setting to be applied will prevail
☐ C. The policy setting highest in the domain heirarchy will be applied
☐ D. The setting lowest in the domain heirarchy will be applied

100. What command-line tool can you use with Windows XP machines to force the update of Group Policy settings that have not already been applied?

☐ A. gpresult
☐ B. gpupdate
☐ C. secedit
☐ D. fdisk

101. Which of the following is the best way to improve the speed of a hard-drive that has just started performing poorly?

☐ A. Defragment it
☐ B. Run Disk Cleanup
☐ C. Make the partitions smaller
☐ D. Delete the paging file

Section A: Exam 70-271
Chapter 5: Troubleshooting Network Protocols and Services

102. What command-line tool can you use to verify the IP address of your computer?

☐ A. ping
☐ B. net
☐ C. ipconfig
☐ D. ifconfig

103. How can you tell if a computer is using APIPA to assign the IP address?

☐ A. The address has the format 169.254.x.x
☐ B. You can verify the IP address of the DHCP server that issued the IP
☐ C. There is no Alternate Configuration option in the IP properties window
☐ D. You are unable to ping the loopback address

104. Which of the following commands can you use to verify connectivity between your computer and a server named SERVER1?

☐ A. ping server1
☐ B. ipconfig server1
☐ C. nslookup server1
☐ D. netstat server1

105. If your computer has both a static and DHCP configuration for the DNS server which one will it use?

☐ A. Neither
☐ B. Both
☐ C. The one from the DHCP Server
☐ D. The static configuration

106. Which of the following commands can you use to verify the MAC address of a remote computer running Windows 2000?

☐ A. ipconfig
☐ B. nbtstat
☐ C. netstat
☐ D. ping

107. You have decided to use the default lmhosts.sam file to do NETBIOS name resolution. Which of the following is required to get this process to work?

☐ A. You must disable the use of WINS
☐ B. You must delete the hosts file
☐ C. The file must be renamed
☐ D. The file must be moved

108. You have decided to start using NETBIOS name resolution on your network. Which of the following files or databases will store your computer names?

☐ A. hosts
☐ B. DNS
☐ C. WINS
☐ D. BIND

109. Which of the following commands will re-register your computer name on your NETBIOS Name Server without rebooting the system?

☐ A. nbtstat -RR
☐ B. nbtstat -r
☐ C. netstat -RR
☐ D. netstat -r

110. To troubleshoot name resolution on a computer you need to know the order in which resources are checked for IP addresses. Of the four files or databases shown below which is checked first when resolving a FQDN?

☐ A. hosts
☐ B. lmhosts
☐ C. DNS
☐ D. WINS

111. You are trying to setup your Windows XP system with an Alternate IP Address configuration but are unable to? Which of the following is a possible reason for this?

☐ A. Your computer is not connected to a network
☐ B. You disabled the NETBIOS protocol on your computer
☐ C. Your computer is using APIPA
☐ D. The machine is configured with a static IP address

112. Your network connects to the Internet through a local Firewall. What option in Internet Explorer must you configure to connect to Internet resources?

☐ A. Proxy Server
☐ B. VPN Client
☐ C. RAS Client
☐ D. Router

113. You need to reconfigure a users computer using Remote Assistance or Remote Desktop before the user comes into the office. What advantage does using Remote Desktop have over using Remote Assistance in this situation?

☐ A. It does not require you to have any permissions on the users computer
☐ B. It does not require the user to be at his computer
☐ C. It does not require Terminal Server to be installed
☐ D. It does not require Administrative rights on the users computer

114. Which of the following would be an invalid IP address to assign to a computer for regular network communications?

☐ A. 10.15.255.0
☐ B. 220.255.1.15
☐ C. 10.255.255.1
☐ D. 224.5.2.90

115. Which of the following commands is used to verify name resolution on a DNS server?

☐ A. nslookup
☐ B. ipconfig
☐ C. ping
☐ D. netstat

116. Which of the following is an authentication protocol that can be used for dial-up connections?

☐ A. PPP
☐ B. SLIP
☐ C. CHAP
☐ D. L2TP

117. Which of the following is a type of VPN tunneling protocol?

☐ A. PPP
☐ B. L2TP
☐ C. SLIP
☐ D. RADIUS

118. Which of the following protocols will provide the highest level of encryption for VPN data?

☐ A. IPSEC
☐ B. SSL
☐ C. MPPE
☐ D. PAP

119. Which of the following protocols will provide the best protection for your username and password when it is sent over a VPN connection?

☐ A. MS-CHAP
☐ B. CHAP
☐ C. PAP
☐ D. SHIVA

120. A user wants to use Multilink for his Dial-up conections from home. Which of the following describes an advantage of using this protocol?

☐ A. It uses a higher level of encryption to increase data transfer
☐ B. It uses a higher level of compression to increase data transfer
☐ C. It uses two or more phone lines to increase data transfer
☐ D. It creates a shared link which allows you to make phone calls will the line is being used for RAS

121. A user has a single network card in his desktop computer but needs to have three IP addresses assigned to his computer for testing an application. Which of the following solutions will do this in the least intrusive way?

☐ A. Assign additional IP addresses to his network card
☐ B. Add additional network cards to the computer
☐ C. Configure his network card to use the multilink protocol
☐ D. Remove the network card and use three modems with the multilink protocol

Section B: Exam 70-272
Chapter 6: Configuring and and Troubleshooting Applications

1. A user wants to be able to assign permissions to files on his hard-drive that has a FAT partition. What must be done before he is able to do this?

☐ A. Convert the file system to NTFS
☐ B. Convert the file system to FAT32
☐ C. Convert the hard-drive to a dynamic disk
☐ D. Convert the partition to a dynamic partition

2. A user needs to be able to share folders on his computer running Windows XP. Which of the following must be done before he can do this?

☐ A. The file system must be converted to NTFS
☐ B. He must install at least Service Pack 1
☐ C. The computer must be the member of a Windows 2000 domain
☐ D. He must be assigned special privileges or be a member of the Administrators or Power Users Group

3. Which of the following methods can you use to verify if an application was written for a 32-bit operating system?

☐ A. If it can be added to the Recycle Bin
☐ B. If checking the properties of the executable file shows a Version folder
☐ C. If the program can be started from the run window
☐ D. If the program can be started from the command-prompt

4. Which of the following statements is true of MS-DOS based applications run in NTVDMs?

☐ A. Each application started will create its own NTVDM
☐ B. Each application started will run in the same NTVDM
☐ C. All such applications will share 16 gigabytes of real memory space
☐ D. All such applications will share 16 gigabytes of virtual memory space

5. Which of the following statements is true of 16-bit applications run on Windows XP systems?

☐ A. They will each work in their own separate NTVDM
☐ B. They must use the same PIF file
☐ C. Windows XP does not support the use of NTVDMs for 16-bit applications
☐ D. They will share the same NTVDM

6. How does a PIF file for a 16-bit application get the settings usually found in autoexec.bat?

☐ A. From the autoexec.bat file in the root of the active partition
☐ B. From the autoexec.nt file in the SYSTEM32 folder
☐ C. From the autoexec.bat file in the SYSTEM32 folder
☐ D. From the autoexec.nt file in the root of the active partition

7. After installing a Windows 98 program on your Windows XP system it is not able to run properly. Which of the following methods should you use to try and fix the problem?

☐ A. Delete the autoexec.bat file from the root of the Active Partition
☐ B. Delete the autoexec.nt file from the root of the Active Partition
☐ C. Try the Program Compatibility Wizard
☐ D. Reinstall the program using the Command Prompt

8. You install a DOS program that requires special startup settings to run properly. The existing autoexec.nt and config.nt files cannot be modified however because of the special needs of other applications. How can you get the new application to run properly?

☐ A. Create customized autoexec.nt and config.nt files and create a shortcut for the application that points to them
☐ B. Save the applications special configuration settings in the registry
☐ C. Rename the existing autoexec.nt and config.nt files and create new ones for the application
☐ D. This cannot be done. All applications must use the same autoexec.nt and config.nt files

9. You are trying to install Office XP on your computer but are unsuccessful. Which of the following is a possible reason for this?

☐ A. You are logged in with a domain account instead of a local one
☐ B. The FAT32 partition has not been converted to NTFS
☐ C. The NTFS partition has not been converted to FAT32
☐ D. Disk Quotas are being enforced on your hard-drive

10. The Dr. Watson program can create error files used to debug application problems. What type of file is this and what is its name?

☐ A. It is a binary file named drwtsn32.log
☐ B. It is a text file named drwtsn32.log
☐ C. It is a text file named watson32.log
☐ D. It is a binary file named watson32.log

11. Which of the following is the best way to schedule regular updates to computers in a workgroup environment?

☐ A. Group Policy
☐ B. SMS
☐ C. Script Files
☐ D. Automatic Updates

12. A user wants to install a DOS application on his Windows XP desktop and asks for your advice. What might you tell him?

☐ A. This cannot be done
☐ B. This will definately work since Windows XP provides for backward compatibility with any DOS application
☐ C. This will work only if the 32-bit version of Windows XP is used
☐ D. This might work depending on how the program works in a NTVDM

13. You are configuring an e-mail client for a user who needs to specify the name of an SMTP server. What is the role of the SMTP server in this configuration?

☐ A. It stores e-mail messages for a user
☐ B. It forwards e-mail messages for a user
☐ C. It creates its own connection to the Internet
☐ D. It uses a Proxy Server to create a connection to the Internet

14. Which of the following protocols can a user use to retrieve e-mail messages from his e-mail server?

☐ A. IMAP
☐ B. SMTP
☐ C. LDAP
☐ D. SNTP

15. What port number is normally used to connect to an SMTP server?

☐ A. 143
☐ B. 119
☐ C. 25
☐ D. 21

16. Which of the following is not a method available to reconfigure Internet Explorer settings for connecting to the Internet?

☐ A. Group Policy
☐ B. Registry
☐ C. IEAK
☐ D. Windows Update

17. A user wants to prevent Internet vendors from tracking her activities on the Internet. Which of the following resources will she configure to control this?

☐ A. Cookies
☐ B. SSL Encryption
☐ C. Temporary Internet Files
☐ D. History

18. A user has four e-mail accounts. One is used for office e-mail and the other three are Internet accounts. Two of those accounts are with the same ISP. How many e-mail profiles are needed to access all his e-mail messages?

☐ A. One
☐ B. Two
☐ C. Three
☐ D. Four

19. You are configuring an e-mail client to retrieve information from an NNTP server. What port number will you use to connect to this server?

☐ A. 143
☐ B. 119
☐ C. 21
☐ D. 23

20. You are running out of room on your hard-drive and need to delete some files immediately. Which of the following categories of files would you delete first?

☐ A. Temporary Internet Files
☐ B. All files in the System folder without a DLL extension
☐ C. User Profiles
☐ D. All compressed files

21. Which of the following can you use to prevent the installation of specific applications on desktops in a domain environment?

☐ A. Windows Update
☐ B. Internet Explorer Security Settings
☐ C. Group Policy
☐ D. Automatic Updates

22. After an administrator installs an application on a computer the user is unable to run the program. The administrator was able to run the program before logging off. What could be causing this problem?

☐ A. The rights and permissions of the user
☐ B. The application was not installed properly
☐ C. The application is not compatible with Windows XP
☐ D. The computer needs the latest service pack

23. A user asks you to configure Fast User Switching on his desktop so that his logon process will be similar to what he does at home with his Windows XP Home Edition computer. He wants to do it without affecting other systems on the network. What can you tell the user about Fast User Switching?

☐ A. It can only be used on the Home Edition of XP
☐ B. It can only be used in a Workgroup Environment
☐ C. It can work in a domain but only if Group Policy settings are disabled.
☐ D. It can be done for a single computer

24. A user wants to prevent a web-site from using information in cookies not generated by it. What is the best way to do this without unduly limiting the functionality of your browser?

☐ A. Disable all cookies
☐ B. Disable the use of Third-party cookies
☐ C. Disable the use of First-party cookies
☐ D. Elevate the security settings on your firewall

25. How can a user lower the security requirements for Internet web-sites he trusts without changing these settings for other sites?

☐ A. Change the Trusted Sites settings under Security in Internet Explorer Options
☐ B. Change the Restricted Sites settings under Security in Internet Explorer Options
☐ C. Change the Internet settings under Security in Internet Explorer Options
☐ D. Disable the use of cookies on all sites except for the ones that you specify

26. You have been asked to enable the Content Advisor option in Internet Explorer on two users computers. They first of all want a description of how it works. Which of the following statements is true of the Content Advisor configuration?

☐ A. It affects all users who log into the machine
☐ B. You can customize the types of content to block e.g. News or E-commerce
☐ C. Any user with a valid logon can configure it
☐ D. Once enabled there is no provision to allow access to unrated sites

27. You want to encrypt web traffic between your computer and the web-site of a vendor. How does your computer verify the Identity of the web server before doing this?

☐ A. Cookies
☐ B. IP Address
☐ C. Certificates
☐ D. MAC Address

28. A user has disabled the use of all certificates on his computer. How will this affect his Internet browsing experience?

☐ A. He will not be able to fill out forms on the Internet
☐ B. He will not be able to send any e-mail messages
☐ C. He will not be able to receieve Internet e-mail messages
☐ D. He will not be abe to connect to secure web-sites using HTTPS

29. What feature of Internet Explorer allows you to fill out web forms without re-typing information that you have used on previous forms?

☐ A. Content Advisor
☐ B. AutoComplete
☐ C. History
☐ D. Temporary Internet Files

30. A user asks for your help to configure Internet Explorer to save the password he uses for an Internet web-site. What can you tell the user?

☐ A. This feature is only available for administrators
☐ B. This can only be done with Intranet Web-sites
☐ C. The computer needs at least Service Pack 2 for this feature to work
☐ D. This can be done using the AutoComplete option

31. Which of the following actions must be done before you can make a web-site available for offline access?

☐ A. Add it to your Favorites
☐ B. Enable cookies
☐ C. Configure it as a Restricted Site
☐ D. Configure it as a Trusted Site

32. Which of the following actions must you perform before deleting a synchronized web page?
☐ A. Disable all Cookies
☐ B. Delete all Favorites
☐ C. Delete the web-site from your Favorites
☐ D. Delete Temporary Inernet Files

33. Which of the following configuration options is not available when setting up Outlook Express?

☐ A. Connecting to POP3 Server
☐ B. Connecting to SMTP Server
☐ C. Connecting to Microsoft Exchange Server
☐ D. Connecting to IMAP Server

34. Which of the following features is available when configuring Outlook Express?

☐ A. Multiple Address Books
☐ B. Contacts
☐ C. Tasks
☐ D. Notes

35. Outlook Express stores e-mails in files using what extension?

☐ A. mdb
☐ B. oex
☐ C. dbx
☐ D. oes

36. Besides using Outlook Express what other way is there to create Identities?

☐ A. Address Book
☐ B. Synchronization Wizard
☐ C. Windows Explorer
☐ D. Active Directory Users and Computers

37. You are looking for the Windows Address Book saved on a users flash drive. Which of the following files is most likely the one you are looking for?

☐ A. data.wab
☐ B. contacts.ab
☐ C. address.win
☐ D. data.add

38. Which of the following describes a service provided by Outlook Express but not available using Outlook?

☐ A. Using Calendars
☐ B. Using Contacts
☐ C. Access to Newsgroups
☐ D. Configuring Access to e-mail using POP3

39. Which of the following is not a protocol used by Outlook Express to provide access to services?

☐ A. POP3
☐ B. SNTP
☐ C. NNTP
☐ D. IMAP

40. Which of the following port numbers is used by Outlook Express to connect to a News Server?

☐ A. 119
☐ B. 143
☐ C. 25
☐ D. 110

Section B: Exam 70-272
Chapter 7: Resolving Issues Related to Usability

41. What tool would you use to configure multi-language support on your system?

☐ A. Component Services
☐ B. Regional and Language Options
☐ C. Computer Management
☐ D. Local Security Policy

42. You need to create a new hardware profile for your laptop to use it at home without its docking station. Which tool can you use to do this?

☐ A. Hardware Wizard
☐ B. Local Security Policy
☐ C. System Properties
☐ D. Disk Management

43. You want to install the latest updates to Microsoft Office Word 2003. What is the best way to get access to this information?

☐ A. Use Windows Update in your Start Menu
☐ B. Use Automatic Updates
☐ C. Use the Check for Updates option under Help in the Word application
☐ D. Use the Online Updates option in Add/Remove Programs

44. You want to configure the Microsoft Office Word 2003 application on your computer to create documents that are more compatible with Word 2000. What is one way that this can be done?

☐ A. In Word 2003 use Tools > Options > Compatibility
☐ B. Install the Word 2000 mst file on your computer
☐ C. Install the Word 2000 msi file on your computer
☐ D. Install the Word 2003 dictionary on the computer running Word 2000

45. You need your Microsoft Office applications to save files you are working on automatically every 5 minutes. Which option must you configure to do this?

☐ A. Task Scheduler
☐ B. File Synchronization
☐ C. AutoSave
☐ D. AutoRecover

46. You want Word 2003 to ignore capitalized words when it does a spell check on your documents. How should this be done?

☐ A. On the menu bar go to Customize > Spelling & Grammar
☐ B. On the menu bar go to Tools > Options > Spelling & Grammar
☐ C. Add all the capitalized words that you use to the customized dictionary
☐ D. Delete the document template used by Word 2003 and replace it with the default one from the installation CD

47. A user wants to disable the offline access of a web-site in Internet Explorer. How can this be done?

☐ A. Change the properties of the web-site link in Favorites
☐ B. Delete Temporary Internet Files
☐ C. Delete all files and folders from the Recycle Bin
☐ D. Disable and Re-enable your network card

48. You want to clear the list of all web-sites you have previously visited from Internet Explorer. Which of the following options will do this?
☐ A. Close and re-open the browser
☐ B. Disable and then Re-enable Offline File Access
☐ C. Clear History
☐ D. Delete Temporary Internet Files

49. You want to configure Internet Explorer to automatically delete the list of names for web-sites you have browsed in the past. Only names that have been in the list for five days or more should be removed. How can you do this?

☐ A. Modify the History settings in Tools > Internet Options > General
☐ B. Modify the Temporary Internet Files settings in Tools > Internet Options > General
☐ C. Modify the Offline Files Properties
☐ D. Modify the properties of the Recycle Bin

50. A user is working on a computer where Internet Explorer is in Full-Screen mode and he is not able to access the menu options. How can he quickly reconfigure it so he can work with the menu options?

☐ A. Press F11
☐ B. Press Enter
☐ C. Press F10
☐ D. Press F12

51. You need to import an Address book into Outlook Express. What extension will the address book file likely have?

☐ A. dbx
☐ B. wab
☐ C. mdb
☐ D. xls

52. A user asks you to configure Outlook Express to use a second address book that holds personal information in addition to the one it is already using. How can you help this user?

☐ A. Use the parameters in Tools > Options > Maintenance
☐ B. Use the parameters in Tools > Options > General
☐ C. Use the Import Wizard
☐ D. Tell the user it cannot be done

Section B: Exam 70-272
Chapter 8: Resolving Issues Related to Application Customization

53. You need to configure your browser to perform Integrated Windows Authentication. How can this be done?

☐ A. Modify the Internet Options in Internet Explorer
☐ B. Modify the Local Computer Security Policy
☐ C. Modify the Regional and Language Options
☐ D. Modify your TCP/IP configuration

54. You need to limit the amount of space used on your hard-drive for Temporary Internet Files. Where can this be done?

☐ A. In the Hardware folder of System Properties
☐ B. In the Internet Options of Internet Explorer
☐ C. In the Disk Management Tool
☐ D. In Windows Explorer

55. A user wants to activate his copy of Office 2003 for his home computer but does not have an Internet connection. What is his next best option?

☐ A. Activate it by telephone
☐ B. Bring it into the office for activation
☐ C. Disable activation in the Help menu of any Office 2003 product
☐ D. Reinstall Office 2003 and disable activation in the Install Wizard

56. You need to automate the installation of Office 2003 on the computers in your network. You have an Active Directory domain of which all the client computers are members and they all run Windows XP. Which of the following methods will accomplish the automated install?

☐ A. Windows Update
☐ B. Automatic Updates
☐ C. Group Policy
☐ D. DFS

57. A user on your network has gone on a three week business project which might turn into months. He calls to tell you that the copy of Office 2003 on his computer was not activated before he left on the trip. He periodically connects to the office through a VPN connection but you will not be able to work on his system until he comes back. What should you advise him to do?

☐ A. Take the laptop to your office as soon as he gets back
☐ B. Do the Activation himself over the Internet
☐ C. Try to launch Office less than 50 times
☐ D. Uninstall Office 2003 and reinstall it for him when he comes back to the office

58. During the initial install of Office 2003 on your desktop you did not install Access. You have now changed your mind and need to install. How should this be done?

☐ A. By customizing the Office install from Add/Remove Programs
☐ B. Uninstall and Reinstall Office 2003
☐ C. Use the Upgrade CD to add the additional components
☐ D. Use the Resource Kit CD to add the additional components

59. A user mistakenly deletes some DLL files needed to run Office 2003 products. What is the easiest way to replace these files?

☐ A. Reinstall Office 2003 from the CD
☐ B. Reinstall Office 2003 from Add/Remove Programs
☐ C. Upgrade Office 2003 from Add/Remove Programs
☐ D. Repair Office 2003 from Add/Remove Programs

60. You are working on an important document in Word 2003 when the application freezes and you are unable to save your changes. What is the best way to make sure that you recover as much of the document as possible?

☐ A. Use the Microsoft Office Application Recovery tool
☐ B. Use Task Manager
☐ C. Use AutoRecover
☐ D. Use Shadow Copy

61. A user has accidentally deleted an important department document from a network share and needs to restore the document as it existed the evening before. Which of the following methods will do this most efficiently?

☐ A. Tape Restore
☐ B. Offline-Files
☐ C. Shadow Copy Restore
☐ D. Disk Mirroring

62. A user has accidentally deleted a file from his local hard-drive and needs to restore it. Which of the following methods will do this most efficiently?

☐ A. Shadow Copies
☐ B. Offline Files
☐ C. Tape Restore
☐ D. System Restore

63. One of your users is unable to add a new word to his custom dictionary in Word 2003. What is one possible reason for this?

☐ A. The dictionary has too many words
☐ B. The word was misspelled
☐ C. The word is capitalized
☐ D. The word has non-alphabetic characters in it

64. What feature of Office applications will automatically fix incorrectly typed words?

☐ A. AutoSummarize
☐ B. AutoCorrect
☐ C. Spell Checker
☐ D. AutoRecover

65. A user is trying to modify the location and size of the toolbars in Internet Explorer but is unable. What is one possible reason for this?

☐ A. You are not logged in as an Administrator
☐ B. You have not installed Internet Explorer Service Pack 1
☐ C. You have not installed Windows XP Service Pack 1
☐ D. The toolbars are locked

66. Which of the following menu options will allow you to modify the toolbars used in a Microsoft Office 2003 product?

☐ A. Tools > Toolbars
☐ B. Insert > Toolbars
☐ C. View > Toolbars
☐ D. Edit > Toolbars

67. A user is searching for his personal folder file from Outlook using Windows Explorer. What file extension should he look for?

☐ A. ost
☐ B. pst
☐ C. dbx
☐ D. xml

68. You need to configure a users Outlook client on his laptop to use RPC over HTTP when accessing e-mail. Which of the following is required for this configuration to work?

☐ A. A Windows 2000 Active Directory Domain
☐ B. An Internet Connection
☐ C. Exchange Server 2000
☐ D. Outlook 2003

69. You are helping a user who wants to access his corporate e-mail over the Internet using Outlook 2003. How can this be done without using a VPN connection?

☐ A. Enable IPSec
☐ B. Use SSL
☐ C. Configure RPC over HTTP
☐ D. Install SMTP on the client computer

70. You need to fix an Outlook Personal Folder file for one of your users. Which of the following commands can you use to do this?

☐ A. pstscan
☐ B. outscan
☐ C. rpcping
☐ D. scanpst

71. A user is unable to access some of his e-mail messages from a computer he logs into. When he logs into his original computer all the messages are where they should be in Outlook. What could be causing this problem?

☐ A. The e-mail profile on the second computer is corrupt
☐ B. Some of his messages are stored in a Personal Folder file
☐ C. He is logged into both machines at the same time
☐ D. He is using a roaming profile

72. You want to configure your Outlook client to automatically delete messages that are more than 30 days old. What feature will allow you to do this?

☐ A. AutoArchive
☐ B. AutoRecover
☐ C. AutoDelete
☐ D. AutoSchedule

73. You want to configure rules to manage your incoming e-mails more efficiently. Which of the following statements is not true of using rules in Outlook 2003?

☐ A. They can forward messages to another e-mail account
☐ B. They can support all client protoocol connection types
☐ C. They can notify you of incoming mail
☐ D. They can move messages between folders

74. You are reconfiguring the e-mail profile of a user and need to locate their Personal Address Book on the computer. What file extension will this file have?

☐ A. ost
☐ B. pst
☐ C. pab
☐ D. mdb

75. A user wants to be able to use his personal address book and the corporate one when he works in an Outlook profile. What can you tell him about this configuration?

☐ A. It cannot be done
☐ B. It is only supported for Outlook connections to Microsoft Exchange Server 2003
☐ C. The personal address book must be in an Access database
☐ D. He can import the address book and use it along side the existing corporate one

76. You want to configure RPC over HTTP in Outlook 2003 for e-mail access over the Internet. Which of the following requirements must be in place for this to work?

☐ A. You must be running Windows XP with at least Service Pack 1 and appropriate hotfixes
☐ B. Your computer must have two network cards
☐ C. The VPN client must be configured to use L2TP
☐ D. The VPN client must be configured to use IPSec

77. You need to configure an Outlook profile to cache e-mails on the client computer. The e-mail messages must not be removed from the server and you want automatic synchronization periodically. What option will allow you to configure these features?

☐ A. AutoRecover
☐ B. Cached Exchange Mode
☐ C. AutoArchive
☐ D. Temporary Internet Files

Section B: Exam 70-272
Chapter 9: Configuring and Troubleshooting Connectivity for Applications

78. Which of the following name resolution methods uses a text file that has NETBIOS names to IP address mappings?

☐ A. lmhosts
☐ B. hosts
☐ C. DNS
☐ D. WINS

79. Which of the following tools can you use to troubleshoot problems with DNS name resolution?

☐ A. pathping
☐ B. ping
☐ C. nslookup
☐ D. ipconfig

80. Which of the following UNC paths will connect you to a share named DATA2 on a server named SQLTWO in a domain named ABCMAPS?

☐ A. \\SQLTWO\DATA2
☐ B. \\DATA2\SQLTWO
☐ C. \\ABCMAPS\DATA2
☐ D. \\ABCMAPS\SQLTWO\DATA2

81. Your computer is having trouble resolving names and you want to verify the IP address of your DNS server. Which of the following commands can you use to do this?

☐ A. ipconfig
☐ B. ping
☐ C. pathping
☐ D. tracert

82. Your system is unable to resolve the IP of a web server on your network. You have verified that the DNS server has the correct information for this computer. Which of the following name resolution methods is likely causing this problem?

☐ A. lmhosts
☐ B. WINS Server
☐ C. Broadcast
☐ D. hosts

83. Which of the following commands can you use to verify the MAC address of a Windows XP computer on another subnet in your network?

☐ A. arp
☐ B. pathping
☐ C. ping
☐ D. nbtstat

84. After running ipconfig on a computer it displays a subnet of 0.0.0.0. What might cause this problem?

☐ A. The computer has two network cards
☐ B. Another computer has the same IP address
☐ C. The network card is running a second protocol in addition to TCP/IP
☐ D. The IP address has not been registered on the DNS Server

85. Which of the following commands will force your computer to register its name on the DNS server?

☐ A. ipconfig /release
☐ B. ipconfig /renew
☐ C. ipconfig /registerdns
☐ D. ipconfig /flushdns

86. Which of the following commands will force your computer to remove the IP address it received from a DHCP server?

☐ A. dhcpcmd /flushdns
☐ B. dhcpcmd /release
☐ C. ipconfig /flushdns
☐ D. ipconfig /release

87. After checking the IP configuration on a computer you find that it has an address of 169.254.34.16. Which of the following might you assume from this information?

☐ A. The subnets have too many computers
☐ B. The WINS Server is down
☐ C. The DNS Server is down
☐ D. The DHCP server has no more available IP addresses

88. You have been asked to configure the default gateway on a computer that has an IP address of 192.168.17.54 and a subnet mask of 255.255.255.0. Which of the following addresses could work as the default gateway?

☐ A. 255.255.255.1
☐ B. 192.168.17.50
☐ C. 198.162.17.1
☐ D. 192.168.17.54

89. A user has a computer with two network cards one of which is permantently connected to the Internet. He wants to share this connection with three other machines on his network using ICS. Where should this be done?

☐ A. On the NIC card not connected to the Internet
☐ B. On the NIC card connected to the Internet
☐ C. Internet Explorer on the Connections tab in Internet Options
☐ D. Control Panel using Add/Remove Programs

90. You need to configure your firewall to allow the forwarding of e-mail messages using SMTP. What port number will you be openning up to do this?

☐ A. 553
☐ B. 143
☐ C. 25
☐ D. 21

91. After configuring a VPN client you successfully connect to the VPN server. You are unable to connect to any resources on the network however. What could be the cause of this problem?

☐ A. The DHCP Server is down
☐ B. The Domain Controller is down
☐ C. The level of encryption used to connect to the VPN Server is too high
☐ D. The level of encryption used to connect to the VPN Server is too low

92. Your VPN Server requires clients to use a tunneling protocol that provides the highest level of encryption using IPSEC. Which of the following protocols meets these criteria?

☐ A. PPTP
☐ B. PPP
☐ C. L2TP
☐ D. SLIP

93. You need to configure your network firewall to allow traffic for the Remote Desktop application. What port number will you need to open?

☐ A. 3289
☐ B. 3389
☐ C. 21
☐ D. 4000

94. While trying to print a document in Microsoft Word you get a message indication that you were unable to connect to it. The printer is connected via a USB hub that also connects the USB keyboard you are using. Which of the following is a possible reason for the printer problem?

☐ A. The driver installed for the hub is incorrect
☐ B. The Printer is turned off
☐ C. The USB hub is turned off
☐ D. The wrong printer driver is installed

95. You connect a flash drive to a USB port on your computer but are unable to have the system recognize it. You have not changed the configuration of your computer and were able to get a USB keyboard to work on the same port yesterday. What is one possible reason for this issue?

☐ A. The flash drive is damaged
☐ B. The USB Device has not been enabled in the BIOS of the computer
☐ C. The USB port has not been enabled in the BIOS of the computer
☐ D. The USB port is configured to only support keyboards and mouse

96. The local printer on your system is connected by means of a USB Hub which also connects the keyboard and two other devices to your computer. Sometimes you have trouble printing documents and believe its because of the overloaded Hub. Which of the following would be the best solution to this problem?

☐ A. Connect the keyboard to the computer using its own USB port
☐ B. Connect the printer to the computer using its own USB port
☐ C. Update the drivers for the USB Hub
☐ D. Update the drivers for the printer

97. Which of the following tools would work best for testing connectivity problems between your Outlook client and Exchange Server?

☐ A. ping
☐ B. rpcping
☐ C. pathping
☐ D. tracert

Section B: Exam 70-272
Chapter 10: Configuring Application Security

98. Your manager has instructed you to create a share but to hide it so it is not browsable on the network. How can you do this?

☐ A. Put a $ sign at the beginning of the share name
☐ B. Unpublish the share name from the computer
☐ C. Unpublish the share name from Active Directory
☐ D. Put a $ sign at the end of the share name

99. Your system is running an unauthorized program that replicates itself and tries to propogate through the network using your e-mail client. How is this type of attack often classified?

☐ A. Virus
☐ B. Buffer Overflow
☐ C. Network Spoofing
☐ D. Man-in-the-Middle

100. You need to make the Microsoft Office applications more secure on your desktops. Which of the following configuration settings would give you the most concern?

☐ A. AutoCorrect
☐ B. Fonts
☐ C. Toolbars
☐ D. Macros

101. A user is unable to access any of his encrypted files on the local hard-drive. Which of the following reasons is a possible cause for this?

☐ A. He has recently changed his password
☐ B. His password has been reset
☐ C. You just installed a new service pack
☐ D. Office 2003 has not been activated in the last 50 launches of it

102. A user wants to password protect a confidential Microsoft Word document that he is working on. What can you tell the user to help him protect the file?

☐ A. Enable EFS
☐ B. Use Windows Explorer to modify the properties of the file
☐ C. Use Microsoft Word to modify the properties of the file
☐ D. Password protection is no longer available. He must encrypt the file.

103. A user working with Microsoft Word 2000 on his Windows XP desktop wants to be able to encrypt documents he is working with. The files must be accessible from other document editors such as Wordpad. What can you tell him about doing this?

☐ A. He can do this as long as the file is saved on an NTFS drive
☐ B. He must upgrade to Microsoft Word 2003
☐ C. He must ensure he has the latest updates for Microsoft Word 2000 installed
☐ D. He will only be able to encrypt local and not network files in that version of Microsoft Word

104. You need to find out who is modifying a confidential department file from a share on a domain server. You enable auditing on the server to accomplish this. Where can the log information generated by this audit be found?

☐ A. In the System Log
☐ B. In the Directory Services Log
☐ C. In the Security Log
☐ D. In the Application Log

105. A new user has just been added to a domain group to give him access to a network share. He is still unable to connect to the UNC path however. What should the user do to solve this problem?

☐ A. Delete his profile and create a new one
☐ B. Log off and logon again
☐ C. Reset his password
☐ D. Refresh the Windows Explorer screen

106. You need to give a user access to a network printer using her domain account. The printer is connected to a domain server running Windows Server 2003. What tool can you use to do this?

☐ A. Computer Management
☐ B. Printer Wizard
☐ C. Add/Remove Hardware
☐ D. Active Directory Users and Computers

107. You need access to another users encrypted file. What must be done for you to be able to read this document?

☐ A. You must change the NTFS permissions of the file
☐ B. The user must change the NTFS permissions of the file
☐ C. You must change the list of encryption users
☐ D. The user must change the list of encryption users

108. You are trying to connect to a share named DATA2 on SERVER1 which is a member server in the CLASSROOM5.COM domain. What UNC what would you use to connect to this share?

☐ A. \\SERVER1\DATA2
☐ B. \\CLASSROOM5\DATA2
☐ C. \\DATA2\SERVER1
☐ D. \\DATA2\CLASSROOM5

109. Some confidential company information might have been compromised in an attack on a managers computer. There is a high probability that the system is virus infected. Which of the following tasks will you NOT do before an investigation is finished?

☐ A. Backup the hard-drive
☐ B. Perform a virus scan
☐ C. Disconnect the computer from the network
☐ D. Format the hard-drive

110. All the desktop computers in your network are members of a Windows 2000 domain and running Windows XP. One of your users is unable to encrypt files on his system. No other user has this problem. What is a probable reason for this users problem?

☐ A. A Group Policy setting applied to all Computers in the domain
☐ B. A Group Policy setting applied to all Users in the domain
☐ C. A Local Computer Policy applied on his system
☐ D. A Service Pack update has not been applied to his computer as yet

111. Two conflicting Group Policies have been applied in Active Directory. One installs an accounting program and the other prevents its instalation. How will Active Directory resolve this conflict?

☐ A. The first policy in the heirarchy will have its settings applied
☐ B. The last policy in the heirarchy will have its settings applied
☐ C. The policy with the higher priority setting will be applied
☐ D. The policy with the lower priority setting will be applied

112. You want to implement new security settings to force all Windows XP systems in your workgroup to use IPSec when communicating with each other. What is the best way to configure this?

☐ A. Group Policy
☐ B. VPN Client Security Settings
☐ C. Local Security Policy
☐ D. Internet Explorer Security Settings

113. You want to control access to a confidential department Word document. You need to give some managers the ability to modify it and all other users the ability to read it. The document is on a FAT32 partition. What is the best way to accomplish this?

☐ A. Use the Microsoft Word application to assign a Read password and a separate Modify password
☐ B. Assign appropriate permissions on the file
☐ C. Encrypt the file and assign encryption certificates to each department user
☐ D. This cannot be done

114. You need to reconfigure Internet access for users on your network to prevent everyone except users in the Legal department from using the NetMeeting application. Where is the best location to configure these settings?

☐ A. NetMeeting Application
☐ B. Proxy Server
☐ C. Router
☐ D. Internet Explorer

115. You are troubleshooting a computer that is not able to communicate with desktops on foreign subnets. You can communicate successfully with other computers on the local subnet. What network setting is most likely causing this problem?

☐ A. DNS
☐ B. Subnet Mask
☐ C. WINS
☐ D. Default Gateway

116. You need to start keeping a log of how a color printer on your network is being used. What audit policy must you enable to do this?

☐ A. Privelege Use
☐ B. Directory Service Access
☐ C. Object Access
☐ D. System Events

117. Some new security settings have been applied through Active Directory to your desktop and you want them to take effect immediately without rebooting the system. Which of the following tools will do this?

☐ A. gpupdate
☐ B. gpresult
☐ C. sigverif
☐ D. ipconfig

118. You need to confirm how Active Directory policies are being applied to a computer to fix a recurring problem with it. What command-line tool will show you the policy settings on the machine in a single report?

☐ A. gpupdate
☐ B. gpresult
☐ C. csvde
☐ D. ldifde

119. You want to create a batch file to be used as a logon script to automate the encryption of a folder on everyones C: drive. What command line tool can you use in this batch file to do the encryption?

☐ A. compact
☐ B. compress
☐ C. cipher
☐ D. encrypt

120. A user is trying to encrypt a file on his Windows XP computer that is a member of a Workgroup. What is one possible reason for his inability to encrypt the file?

☐ A. The partition is FAT32
☐ B. The computer is not in a domain
☐ C. He did not login as an Administrator
☐ D. He does not own the file

Appendix A: Answers for Exam 70-271

1. What configuration file contains information about the boot order of operating systems on a desktop?

Answer: A. boot.ini.
Explanation: The boot.ini file contains references to all operating systems your desktop can boot to and the wait time before it loads the default operating system.

2. What is the name of the setup program used to install Windows XP on a system that had no previous operating system?

Answer: D. winnt.exe.
Explanation: winnt32.exe is used for upgrades and winnt.exe is used for regular installations. They are both found in the i386 folder on the install CD.

3. What command would you use to upgrade Windows 2000 to XP if you are doing a manual installation?

Answer: B. winnt32.exe.
Explanation: Winnt32.exe is always used for upgrades.

4. What parameter is used to do an unattended install on a desktop with no previous operating system?

Answer: A. winnt.exe /u.
Explanation: The /u parameter is used with winnt.exe for clean installs. /unattend is used for upgrades using the winnt32.exe command.

5. When doing an unattended install with the /s parameter what

information are you giving?

Answer: C. The path to the setup files.
Explanation: The /s parameter designates the location of the setup files. E.g. e:\i386

6. After doing an installation you decide to install the latest service pack. What must you do to ensure that all previous updates will also be included?

Answer: D. Nothing..
Explanation: Later service packs will include the fixes defined in earlier ones

7. You will be performing unattended setups on twelve computers using a preconfigured answer file. What other file is needed for this procedure to work?

Answer: A. udf.
Explanation: Uniqueness Database Files (UDF) have unique information for each of the machines to be installed

8. What configuration file will contain information about all the operating systems configured on a multi-boot system?

Answer: D. boot.ini.
Explanation: boot.ini will have the path to the boot files for all operating systems recognized by the Windows boot loader

9. What is the minimum RAM configuration for a computer that will be upgraded to Windows XP?

Answer: B. 64MB.
Explanation: The online documentation from Microsoft requires a minimum of 64MB of RAM to support Windows XP

10. You install windows XP on a computer that designates the C: drive as the active partition. The operating system files were installed at D:WINDOWS. The only drive configured as NTFS is the E: drive. The largest partition is 20 GB and designated as F:. Which of these drives is the system partition?

Answer: A. C.
Explanation: The system partition is the location of the bootstrap files that are located on the first active partition.

11. Which of the following command can you use to create a partition?
Answer: D. Fdisk.
Explanation: Of the listed commands only fdisk can create or delete partitions

12. How can you create Windows XP boot disk to start the setup process for a computer?

Answer: B. Download them from the Microsoft Web-Site.
Explanation: Boot disks for Windows XP can only be downloaded from their web-site

13. Which of the following commands would work best for backing up user profile information to be used on another system?

Answer: A. scanstate.
Explanation: Scanstate is used to backup user profiles. Loadstate is used to restore them to a desktop.

14. You have upgraded desktops running Windows 95, Windows NT 4.0 and Windows 2000 to Windows XP. Which of these platforms can be restored to their previous confiiguration by uninstalling Windows XP?

Answer: A. None of them.

Explanation: Only Windows 98 or Millenium can be restored by uninstalling the upgrade to Windows XP.

15. You are configuring a multi-boot system that will be running Windows 98; Windows NT 4.0; Windows 2000 and XP for testing purposes. What is the minimum number of partitions necessary to support this configuration?

Answer: A. One.
Explanation: If you will be using a FAT partition for all the systems then only one partition will be necessary.

16. In a boot.ini file what does a configuration where multi(1) is stated mean?

Answer: D. The operating system is on a drive controlled by the second disk controller.
Explanation: Multi usually refers to the non-scsi disk controller that has the boot files. The numbering starts at zero (0). One (1) would therefore represent the second controller card.

17. On a system that uses only IDE controllers what does the disk(1) parameter mean in a boot.ini file?

Answer: A. Nothing.
Explanation: disk in the boot.ini ARC path is always in reference to a SCSI hard-drive and the number would be ignored for IDE devices.

18. Your computer runs three operating systems with Windows 2000 being the default one loaded at boot time. What tool or file can you use to make Windows XP the default operating system?

Answer: C. boot.ini.
Explanation: The boot.ini file list all the operating systems your computer can boot to and you can change the ARC path for the default

operating system using the information in it.

19. You want to perform a CD based install of Windows XP on a system that does not have a bootable CD-ROM. Which of the following solutions would solve this problem?

Answer: A. Use a Windows 98 boot disk to gain access to the CD-ROM and start the install from there..
Explanation: When you start the computer with a Windows 98 boot disk you will have access to the CD-ROM. You can then install Windows XP using the winnt.exe setup program in the I386 folder.

20. You connect a computer to your network using a MS-DOS 6.22 network boot disk to start the install of Windows XP. It is not able to see the C: drive however which is formatted as a 2 Gigabyte FAT32 partition. Why can the boot disk not see the C: drive?

Answer: D. DOS does not recognize FAT32 partitions.
Explanation: The earliest Windows O.S. that recognizes FAT32 is Windows 98. Earlier operating systems will not work with it.

21. You have an 8 gigabyte partition on a system where you will install Windows XP. Which of the following file systems can you use to start the unattended install?

Answer: B. FAT32.
Explanation: Unattended installs must be done on FAT or FAT32 partitions. However, the maximum size of a FAT partition is only 4 gigabytes.

22. What is the function of smartdrv.exe on a MS-DOS startup disk?

Answer: C. It improves the speed of file copy operations.
Explanation: Smartdrv.exe is used to cache copied files in memory to

speed up the operation.

23. Which log file generated by the Windows XP setup process will give information about errors detected during install?

Answer: B. setuperr.log.
Explanation: The setup process records errors in the setuperr.log file

24. Which of the following files will record tasks that were performed during the Windows XP setup process?

Answer: A. setuplog.txt.
Explanation: setuplog.txt can be checked for details about the tasks that were performed during setup.

25. You are doing an unattended setup for twenty (20) new desktops on your network. Their configuration will be identical. Which configuration file will most likely contain the display settings for all the computers?

Answer: A. unattend.txt.
Explanation: The unattend.txt file will contain all settings common to the different desktops.

26. You will be performing an unattended setup for some new machines on your network. Which configuration file will contain the computer names for these machines?

Answer: B. unattend.udf.
Explanation: Uniqueness Database Files (normally named unattend.udf) contain information unique to each machine such as its computer name.

27. You will be configuring a dual boot install on your system thats running Windows 98 on the C: drive. The Windows XP install must

have a secure file system. Which of the following solutions will accomplish this?

Answer: D. Create an additional partition and use NTFS for the XP install on it.
Explanation: To have a secure file system you will need NTFS since Windows 98 does not support it an additional partition is necessary.

28. What tool is used to strip out unique information from a computer before a network image is made of the Operating System?

Answer: A. Sysprep.
Explanation: Sysprep will remove unique information such as the computer name and SID#. Its normally used before creating a disk image.

29. You want to permanently install the Recovery Console on a desktop used for testing. Which of the following commands will do this?

Answer: C. winnt32.exe /cmdcons.
Explanation: winnt32.exe must be used to install the Recovery Console.

30. You are using System Restore to replace corrupted registry files on a computer. A typical install of Windows XP was done on the system. What location should the files be copied to?

Answer: B. c:windows\system32\config.
Explanation: The registry files are stored in c:\windows\system32\config and the replacement files must be put there.

31. If a user belongs to two groups that have access to a folder how is the users effective permissions calculated?

Answer: C. He will get the combined permissions of both groups.
Explanation: Effective permissions on a folder or file are calculated by combining the permissions of all the groups the user belongs to.

32. What command can you use to change a FAT32 partition to NTFS without the loss of any files?

Answer: A. convert.
Explanation: Only the command-line convert.exe command can be used to change a FAT partition to NTFS without loosing any files

33. What can the NTFS modify permission do that the write permission cannot?

Answer: C. Delete a file.
Explanation: NTFS Modify and Write permissions are identical except for the ability to delete included with Modify.

34. In what situation are share permissions used instead of NTFS for network users?

Answer: B. When they are more restrictive.
Explanation: Windows computers will use the more restrictive of NTFS or Share permissions for network users.

35. In what situation will you not be able to assign unique permissions for different groups of users to a share?

Answer: A. If you are using Simple File Sharing.
Explanation: Simple File Sharing allows you to quickly share a folder that will be accessible to anyone on the network

36. Which of the following would prevent you from encrypting a file on your hard-drive?

Answer: B. The file system is FAT32.
Explanation: Encrypting a file using EFS requires that the file system be NTFS

37. Which of the following commands will share the folder C:\TEMP with the name TEMP$?

Answer: D. net share temp=c:\temp.
Explanation: The correct syntax is net share followed by the name of the new share and then the name of the folder being shared.

38. A user has just been added to a group to give him access to a shared resource. What must he do to take advantage of his new permissions?

Answer: C. Logout and login again.
Explanation: His access token needs to be updated with the new information about his group membership. Logging in and out will accomplish this.

39. You are trying to compress some files on your C: drive but are unable to do so. Which of the following could be the cause?

Answer: B. The file system is FAT32.
Explanation: Files on a FAT or FAT32 partition cannot be compressed.

40. Which of the following features cannot be used at the same time as file encryption?

Answer: A. File Compression.
Explanation: You can use either file encyption or compression for files on an NTFS drive but not both at the same time.

41. You are unable to modify the permissions on a folder for a particular group even though you can do this for other groups. What is one possible explanation for this?

Answer: C. The permissions were inherited.
Explanation: Inherited permissions cannot be modified. Only removed entirely.

42. You are trying to share a folder but are unable to do so. Which of the following is a plausible reason for this?

Answer: D. The folder is on a network connected drive.
Explanation: You cannot share folders on a network connected drive.

43. You are assigning permissions to a network share that is on an NTFS drive. How should you assign the permissions?

Answer: C. On NTFS only.
Explanation: Since NTFS gives you greater flexibility in controlling permissions it should be used to control access instead of the share.

44. What command-line tool is used to compress files?

Answer: A. compact.
Explanation: compact is the command-line tool used for compression on NTFS drives

45. What are the effective permissions of a network user who has Full Control on a share but has been denied permissions on NTFS?

Answer: A. He will have no access.
Explanation: Effective permissions will be calculated by taking the more restrictive of the two permissions. He will therefore be denied access.

46. What permissions will a user have to a local folder if his NTFS permissions give him Full Control but its Share permissions deny him access?

Answer: A. Full Control.
Explanation: Share permissions are not applied to a user when he accesses local hard-drive resources so only the NTFS permissions will apply.

47. A user is unable to browse for a particular share on another Windows XP system although the others are accessible. The computer is named COMPUTER23 and the share is named FRIDAY$. What could be causing this problem?

Answer: C. The share is hidden because of the $ sign.
Explanation: Shares with a $ sign at the end are hidden and cannot be browsed on the network.

48. Which of the following tools can you use to enable Offline Files on your computer?

Answer: B. Windows Explorer.
Explanation: Offline Files can be enabled by using the Tools folder in Windows Explorer

49. A user tries to install a local printer but is unable to do so because of his limited privileges. Which of the following local groups will give the user permissions to do this?

Answer: D. Power Users.
Explanation: To add a local printer you need the privileges of the local Administrator or Power Users group.

50. What UNC path will you use to connect to a printer named HP_Laser_Jet if it has a share name of HPLASERJ on a server named

PRINTSERVER1?

Answer: A. \\PRINTERSERVER1\HPLASERJ.
Explanation: The UNC path always includes the server name followed by the share name.

51. Which of the following is a requirement for setting up a printer pool?

Answer: B. All the print devices must be able to use the same driver.
Explanation: Even if all the devices are not identical they must use the same driver

52. You try to enable offline files on your home computer running Windows XP Home Edition but cannot do so. Why is this the case?

Answer: D. This version of XP does not support offline files.
Explanation: The Home Edition of Windows XP does not support offline files.

53. A users My Documents folders has been redirected to a network share. He now asks you to configure his work laptop to automatically keep a copy of the files he works with so he can work from home. What feature configuration on his laptop would best accomplish this?

Answer: D. Enable offline files.
Explanation: Offline files can be configured to cache the files from any network share onto the local hard-drive. It will also automatically synchronize any changes.

54. Which of the following UNC paths points to a hidden share?
Answer: B. \\SERVER1\SHARE0$.
Explanation: A hidden share is created by putting a $ (dollar) sign at the end of the share name. They are described as hidden because they

cannot be browsed on the network like regular shares.

55. How many partitions can you create on a hard-drive if you are running the Windows XP operating system?

Answer: B. Four.
Explanation: Regardless of the O.S. you are running only four partitions can be created on a regular basic disk.

56. You must create six separate drives on a new hard-drive. Which of the following will allow you to accomplish this?

Answer: A. Create an extended partition.
Explanation: Extended paritions can be divided into multiple logical drives unlike primary partitions

57. What is the maximum number of extended partitions that can be created on a hard-drive?

Answer: A. One.
Explanation: Although you can create up to four primary partitions only one extended can be created on a hard-drive.

58. Which of the following is NOT a requirement for mounting a partition to a drive?

Answer: B. The drive you are mounting to must have at least 1 metabyte of drive space free.
Explanation: There is no free space requirement for the mounting drive.

59. Which of the following configuration options will do a complete shutdown of your computer?

Answer: A. Hibernate.

Explanation: Hibernation copies the information in memory to your hard-drive and then shuts down the computer. It is mainly used to conserve power on battery operated laptops.

60. What system component would you use to reconfigure your computer to boot to the CD-ROM media before using the hard-drive on startup?

Answer: B. BIOS.

Explanation: The BIOS on a computer can be used to change the boot order of devices.

61. Which of the following configurations would most likely benefit from the use of a hardware profile?

Answer: C. A laptop with a docking station.

Explanation: A hardware profile is used in environments where the computer system will install drivers for devices that are not connected during some system startups. The objective is to prevent the computer from trying to load a device that will not be there.

62. You want to configure your system to use a multi-monitor configuration by means of three video cards. What is one requirement for these video cards?

Answer: A. They must be PCI or AGP cards.

Explanation: The video cards must be PCI or AGP

63. You are using a multi-monitor configuration on your system. Which of the following statements is not true about configuring such a setup?

Answer: C. The monitors must use the same video resolution.

Explanation: The monitors can be configured to use different screen resolution settings.

64. At what stage in the boot process will you be allowed to choose a hardware profile?

Answer: C. After the Operating System is chosen in the boot loader.
Explanation: If you have multiple hardware profiles the choices are displayed after you choose the operating system to load in the boot loader

65. After installing a new driver for one of your SCSI controllers it no longer works properly. What is the easiest way to get back the older configuration without losing any other system changes?

Answer: B. Driver Roll Back.
Explanation: Using the Driver Roll Back feature will restore the previous working driver without affecting other system settings.

66. Some users on your network have had trouble with software drivers that they install on their systems that cause system crashes. How can you best control this problem without affecting their other privileges?

Answer: A. Configure Driver Signing.
Explanation: When driver signing is configured in Block mode it prevents the installation of any drivers not signed by Microsoft. These have been tested to prevent system instability.

67. Which of the following tools can you use to create a list of all drivers installed on your system?

Answer: B. driverquery.
Explanation: Driveryquery is a new command-line tool for querying

information about installed drivers.

68. You need to reconfigure the default I/O settings for one of the plug-and-play devices on your computer. Where can this be done?

Answer: D. Device Manager.
Explanation: The device manager can be used to modify the I/O and Interrupt settings of devices.

69. Which command-line tool can you use to assign a new driver letter to a partition?

Answer: A. diskpart.
Explanation: Diskpart can be used to create or delete partitions and also change the drive letter assigned to them.

70. A user has asked you to configure the Hibernation and Standby settings for their new laptop. Which of the following statements is true concerning this configuration?
Answer: C. Hibernation will do a complete shutdown of the system.
Explanation: Standby and Hibernation modes are totally independent of each other. Hibernation will completely shutdown the system and copy memory information to your hard-drive while Standby leaves some devices running.

71. After installing an incorrect video driver you decide to boot with a generic VGA driver to fix the problem. Which of the following will accomplish this?

Answer: A. Safe Mode.
Explanation: Safe Mode will load a generic driver. VGA mode loads the existing driver in VGA mode.

72. A user is complaining that the user before changed the video settings and now the items on his screen are too small to read. What

should he do to fix this problem?

Answer: B. Decrease the screen resolution.
Explanation: Decreasing the screen resolution will make the items bigger

73. You are having some trouble getting a new USB device to be recognized by your computer. It is connected to a USB hub and all the five other devices on it are working. What is one possible cause of this problem?

Answer: C. The cable connecting the new device to the USB hub is bad.
Explanation: It is possible that the cable connecting the new device to the hub is bad. All the other suggestions point to the USB hub but the fact that other devices on it are working preclude this.

74. You are trying to configure hibernation on your Windows 2000 Professional desktop computer but are unable to do so. What could be the cause of this problem?

Answer: A. ACPI support was not installed.
Explanation: ACPI allows a systems power settings to be controlled from the operating system. The existence of some legacy devices might prevent its install during the setup of Windows 2000 or XP.

75. You need your laptop to automatically power down the monitor and hard-drive after 30 minutes of inactivity. Which of the following options will allow you to do this?

Answer: B. Power Schemes.
Explanation: By configuring your Power Scheme you can tell the system when to go into Standby Mode to save power by shutting down the monitor and hard-drive.

76. After connecting a USB drive to your system what else must you do to access its resources?

Answer: C. Nothing.
Explanation: Once the USB device is detected its partitions are assigned drive letters and accessible in the same way as local partitions

77. What is one advantage that IEEE 1394 devices have over USB devices?

Answer: A. Speed.
Explanation: Updates to the original USB standards allow for speeds in the hundreds of Mbits/sec while IEEE 1394 updates allow for up to three Gbps.

78. Which of the following commands can you use to create a user account?

Answer: B. net user.
Explanation: The net user command can be used with the /add parameter to create a new account

79. What must a user do to ensure that his profile is not used by another user who logs onto his machine?

Answer: D. Nothing.
Explanation: Each users profile is by default private and will not be used by anyone else logging into his system.

80. A legally blind user needs a way to increase the size of different areas on his screen while working. Which of the following options would help in this situation?

Answer: B. Magnifier.
Explanation: The Magnifier can be used to increase the size of

different areas on your desktop

81. A legally blind user wants a way to identify different options as he works in applications on his desktop. Which of the following options would help?

Answer: D. Narrator.
Explanation: The narrator is an accessibility option that has the computer read off options as they are chosen on the desktop or in an application.

82. What database is used to authenticate local user accounts?

Answer: A. sam.
Explanation: The sam database is located on the local hard-drive of systems to authenticate local user logons

83. How can a user open an application with different credentials from the one he is already logged in with without changing his existing login status?

Answer: B. Secondary Logon.
Explanation: A secondary logon allows you to use a single application with different credentials from the one you logged on with.

84. A user on your local network is unable contact a domain controller for authentication purposes during logon. Which of the following services if improperly configured could be causing this problem?

Answer: D. DNS.
Explanation: DNS is needed to find an appropriate Domain Controller in a domain.

85. Your manager has decided to use multi-factor authentication to ensure more secure logons. Which of the following describes a multi-

factor authentication method available on Windows XP?

Answer: D. Username and Passwords.
Explanation: Smart Card support is built into Windows XP. It is considered a multi-factor authentication method because it involves the use of a card and PIN number. Usernames and passwords is considered single factor because all that is required is information.

86. A user running Windows 2000 wants to create a disk that allows him to reset his password if he forgets it. How can this be done?

Answer: D. It cannot be done..
Explanation: This can be done on Windows XP using a Password Reset Disk but this feature is not available on Windows 2000.

87. Which of the following tools can you use to monitor Processor performance and close applications that eat up too much of your system resources?

Answer: A. Task Manager.
Explanation: System Monitor can be used to monitor the use of the Processor but Task Manager can also be used to end processes and applications.

88. One of the users on your network wants to enable Fast User Switching on her desktop but is unable to do so. What is one possible cause of this problem?

Answer: B. The computer is running Windows 2000.
Explanation: Fast User switching is not available on Windows 2000 only XP.

89. A user is unable to change his configuration to use Fast User Switching and asks for your help. Which of the following might be causing this?

Answer: A. This computer is a member of a domain.
Explanation: Windows XP machines that are members of domains cannot use Fast User Switching

90. Which of the following tools is used to create a domain user account?

Answer: C. Active Directory Users and Computers.
Explanation: AD Users and Computers is used to create and manage user; group and computer accounts.

91. Which of the following tools can you use to reset the password of a local user account?

Answer: D. Computer Management.
Explanation: The Local Users and Groups option is available in Computer Management to manage local user accounts

92. A user wants to have his desktop configuration duplicated on each new computer he logs into so he does not have to reconfigure it each time. What is the best way for you to help him?

Answer: B. Configure a roaming profile for him.
Explanation: A roaming profile allows him to use the same profile regardless of which computer he logs into.

93. A user wants to reconfigure his local user account to have a roaming profile. How can he do this?

Answer: D. It cannot be done..
Explanation: Roaming profiles can only be used with domain user accounts. Roaming profiles allow a user to use the same account settings on multiple machines. A local account only works on one machine.

94. You need to create a profile for a group of users with desktop settings that cannot be permanently changed by them. What type of profile will allow you to do this?

Answer: D. Mandatory.
Explanation: A mandatory profile does not allow a user to permanently change his settings and it can be shared between multiple user accounts.

95. When a user first logs onto a computer from where does his initial profile settings come?

Answer: A. Default User Profile.
Explanation: The Default User Profile acts as a template for all users who log onto a machine. It is only used if they do not already have an existing user profile.

96. Which taskbar toolbar allows you to directly specify web-sites you want to browse?

Answer: A. Address.
Explanation: Address gives you an area like the Address bar in Internet Explorer that allows you to specify the name of a web-site to browse.

97. Which of the following commands will create a group named GROUP1 on your Windows XP desktop?

Answer: B. net localgroup /add group1.
Explanation: A group being created on an XP machine must be a local group and the NET LOCALGROUP /ADD syntax is used to create these.

98. In what order are Group Policy settings applied in a domain environment?

Answer: C. Local Computer > Site > Domain > OU.
Explanation: The default order of policy application is Local Machine; Site; Domain and finally the OUs. The settings are all combined unless there is a conflict.

99. How does Active Directory apply Group Policy settings when they conflict with each other?

Answer: A. The last policy setting to be applied will prevail.
Explanation: Settings from different policies can only be combined when there is no conflict. When there is a conflict the last one to be applied will win.

100. What command-line tool can you use with Windows XP machines to force the update of Group Policy settings that have not already been applied?

Answer: B. gpupdate.
Explanation: gpupdate can be used to update a systems group policy settings without rebooting the system.

101. Which of the following is the best way to improve the speed of a hard-drive that has just started performing poorly?

Answer: A. Defragment it.
Explanation: Defragmenting a drive regularly is a good way to maintain its performance level.

102. What command-line tool can you use to verify the IP address of your computer?

Answer: C. ipconfig.
Explanation: Ipconfig can be used to view the IP and network card configuration

103. How can you tell if a computer is using APIPA to assign the IP address?

Answer: A. The address has the format 169.254.x.x.
Explanation: Automatic Private IP Addressing is used by a DHCP client when it is unable to obtain an IP from a DHCP server. It automatically assigns itself an IP in the format 169.254.x.x

104. Which of the following commands can you use to verify connectivity between your computer and a server named SERVER1?

Answer: A. ping server1.
Explanation: PING is used to test connectivity between computers

105. If your computer has both a static and DHCP configuration for the DNS server which one will it use?

Answer: D. The static configuration.
Explanation: It is possible to configure a network card to use a DHCP server but at the same time configure static IP information for the DNS Server. Static IP configurations will always be taken over conflicting DHCP settings.

106. Which of the following commands can you use to verify the MAC address of a remote computer running Windows 2000?

Answer: B. nbtstat.
Explanation: nbtstat can be used with the -a or -A parameter to get the MAC address of a remote Windows system.

107. You have decided to use the default lmhosts.sam file to do NETBIOS name resolution. Which of the following is required to get this process to work?

Answer: C. The file must be renamed.

Explanation: For windows to use this file it must be renamed to lmhosts. It must not have a file extension.

108. You have decided to start using NETBIOS name resolution on your network. Which of the following files or databases will store your computer names?

Answer: C. WINS.
Explanation: The WINS database centralizes the registration and resolution of NETBIOS names on a network.

109. Which of the following commands will re-register your computer name on your NETBIOS Name Server without rebooting the system?

Answer: A. nbtstat -RR.
Explanation: nbtstat -RR is used to re-register your name and IP on a WINS server without rebooting.

110. To troubleshoot name resolution on a computer you need to know the order in which resources are checked for IP addresses. Of the four files or databases shown below which is checked first when resolving a FQDN?

Answer: A. hosts.
Explanation: The hosts file is checked before all the other resources mentioned.

111. You are trying to setup your Windows XP system with an Alternate IP Address configuration but are unable to? Which of the following is a possible reason for this?

Answer: D. The machine is configured with a static IP address.
Explanation: A static IP configuration removes the option to configure an alternate IP.

112. Your network connects to the Internet through a local Firewall. What option in Internet Explorer must you configure to connect to Internet resources?

Answer: A. Proxy Server.
Explanation: To connect through the Firewall you would specify the internal IP address or name of the Firewall and the port you connect through. The Network Administrator would have that information.

113. You need to reconfigure a users computer using Remote Assistance or Remote Desktop before the user comes into the office. What advantage does using Remote Desktop have over using Remote Assistance in this situation?

Answer: B. It does not require the user to be at his computer.
Explanation: Remote Desktop unlike Remote Assistance does not require the approval of someone working at the computer to initiate a connection.

114. Which of the following would be an invalid IP address to assign to a computer for regular network communications?

Answer: D. 224.5.2.90.
Explanation: 224.5.2.90 is a multicast IP address used only for multicast communications

115. Which of the following commands is used to verify name resolution on a DNS server?

Answer: A. nslookup.
Explanation: nslookup works with many types of DNS servers and can be used to check the records in its database.

116. Which of the following is an authentication protocol that can be used for dial-up connections?

Answer: C. CHAP.
Explanation: CHAP is an authentication protocol that works with Windows and non-Windows clients for RAS and VPN connections.

117. Which of the following is a type of VPN tunneling protocol?

Answer: B. L2TP.
Explanation: L2TP and PPTP are the two tunneling protocols available for Windows XP VPN clients.

118. Which of the following protocols will provide the highest level of encryption for VPN data?

Answer: A. IPSEC.
Explanation: IPSEC is an VPN encryption protocol sometimes used with L2TP connections. It provides for up to 3DES (168-bit) encryption.

119. Which of the following protocols will provide the best protection for your username and password when it is sent over a VPN connection?

Answer: A. MS-CHAP.
Explanation: Of the protocols shown MS-CHAP provides the best protection for authentication data. Also available are MS-CHAPv2 and EAP.

120. A user wants to use Multilink for his Dial-up conections from home. Which of the following describes an advantage of using this protocol?

Answer: C. It uses two or more phone lines to increase data transfer.
Explanation: Multilink is used to combine bandwidth from multiple dial-up connections. This increases data transfer rates.

121. A user has a single network card in his desktop computer but needs to have three IP addresses assigned to his computer for testing an application. Which of the following solutions will do this in the least intrusive way?

Answer: A. Assign additional IP addresses to his network card. Explanation: Multiple IP addresses can be assigned to a single NIC card using the advanced properties

Appendix B: Answers for Exam 70-272

1. A user wants to be able to assign permissions to files on his hard-drive that has a FAT partition. What must be done before he is able to do this?

Answer: A. Convert the file system to NTFS.
Explanation: Permission can only be assigned to individual files if you are running the NTFS file system.

2. A user needs to be able to share folders on his computer running Windows XP. Which of the following must be done before he can do this?

Answer: D. He must be assigned special privileges or be a member of the Administrators or Power Users Group.
Explanation: Sharing a folder requires special privileges on a computer that the Administrator and Power Users Groups have by default

3. Which of the following methods can you use to verify if an application was written for a 32-bit operating system?

Answer: B. If checking the properties of the executable file shows a Version folder.
Explanation: 16-bit applications do not have a Version folder in the properties settings of their executable files.

4. Which of the following statements is true of MS-DOS based applications run in NTVDMs?

Answer: A. Each application started will create its own NTVDM.
Explanation: DOS based applications always run in their own separate

NTVDM and will not share memory or other resources

5. Which of the following statements is true of 16-bit applications run on Windows XP systems?

Answer: D. They will share the same NTVDM.
Explanation: 16-bit applications will share the same NTVDM by default although they can be configured to work in separate ones

6. How does a PIF file for a 16-bit application get the settings usually found in autoexec.bat?

Answer: B. From the autoexec.nt file in the SYSTEM32 folder.
Explanation: The autoexec.nt and config.nt files in %windir%\System32 are the default files used by program information files.

7. After installing a Windows 98 program on your Windows XP system it is not able to run properly. Which of the following methods should you use to try and fix the problem?

Answer: C. Try the Program Compatibility Wizard.
Explanation: The Program Compatibility Wizard will test the program in different configurations to see if it can get it to run properly.

8. You install a DOS program that requires special startup settings to run properly. The existing autoexec.nt and config.nt files cannot be modified however because of the special needs of other applications. How can you get the new application to run properly?

Answer: A. Create customized autoexec.nt and config.nt files and create a shortcut for the application that points to them.
Explanation: All applications do not have to use the same autoexec.nt and config.nt files. Customized ones can be created and an application directed to them.

9. You are trying to install Office XP on your computer but are unsuccessful. Which of the following is a possible reason for this?

Answer: D. Disk Quotas are being enforced on your hard-drive.
Explanation: Disk Quotas prevent you from using more space on your hard-drive than a preset limit. If the application requires more space than the limit the install will fail

10. The Dr. Watson program can create error files used to debug application problems. What type of file is this and what is its name?

Answer: B. It is a text file named drwtsn32.log.
Explanation: Dr. Watson creates a text file named drwtsn32.log. It can also create an optional crash dump file which is in a binary format.

11. Which of the following is the best way to schedule regular updates to computers in a workgroup environment?

Answer: D. Automatic Updates.
Explanation: Important updates can be automated on your system using automatic updates without the need of a domain configuration. Group Policy requires a domain.

12. A user wants to install a DOS application on his Windows XP desktop and asks for your advice. What might you tell him?

Answer: D. This might work depending on how the program works in a NTVDM.
Explanation: Windows XP uses NTVDMs to emulate a DOS environment for these applications. This does not always work however and it must be tested thoroughly.

13. You are configuring an e-mail client for a user who needs to specify the name of an SMTP server. What is the role of the SMTP server in this configuration?

Answer: B. It forwards e-mail messages for a user.
Explanation: SMTP Servers forward e-mail messages to the e-mail server of the intended recipient.

14. Which of the following protocols can a user use to retrieve e-mail messages from his e-mail server?

Answer: A. IMAP.
Explanation: The IMAP protocol can be used to retrieve e-mail messages. It can be used to control the storage and organization of these messages as well.

15. What port number is normally used to connect to an SMTP server?

Answer: C. 25.
Explanation: SMTP connections are normally done on port 25. Some servers use a non-traditional port number for security reasons.

16. Which of the following is not a method available to reconfigure Internet Explorer settings for connecting to the Internet?

Answer: D. Windows Update.
Explanation: Windows Update can be used to download security patches but will not change specific settings used to connect to the Internet.

17. A user wants to prevent Internet vendors from tracking her activities on the Internet. Which of the following resources will she configure to control this?

Answer: A. Cookies.
Explanation: Cookies are used by vendors to track user activity on their own and other web-sites. The Internet Explorer Security and Privacy settings can be configured to control the use of these resources.

18. A user has four e-mail accounts. One is used for office e-mail and the other three are Internet accounts. Two of those accounts are with the same ISP. How many e-mail profiles are needed to access all his e-mail messages?

Answer: A. One.
Explanation: A single e-mail profile can be configured to retrieve all his e-mails from these different accounts

19. You are configuring an e-mail client to retrieve information from an NNTP server. What port number will you use to connect to this server?

Answer: B. 119.
Explanation: NNTPs traditional port number is 119

20. You are running out of room on your hard-drive and need to delete some files immediately. Which of the following categories of files would you delete first?

Answer: A. Temporary Internet Files.
Explanation: Temporary Internet Files sometimes take of large amounts of drive space. They are not needed for the proper functioning of your system and can be deleted at anytime.

21. Which of the following can you use to prevent the installation of specific applications on desktops in a domain environment?

Answer: C. Group Policy.
Explanation: Group Policies can be used to prevent applications from being installed on domain computers.

22. After an administrator installs an application on a computer the user is unable to run the program. The administrator was able to run the program before logging off. What could be causing this problem?

Answer: A. The rights and permissions of the user.
Explanation: Since the program worked for the administrator this is likely a problem caused by the limited access rights of the user.

23. A user asks you to configure Fast User Switching on his desktop so that his logon process will be similar to what he does at home with his Windows XP Home Edition computer. He wants to do it without affecting other systems on the network. What can you tell the user about Fast User Switching?

Answer: D. It can be done for a single computer.
Explanation: Fast User Switching can be done for individual computers in a domain but is considered less secure than the traditional logon method.

24. A user wants to prevent a web-site from using information in cookies not generated by it. What is the best way to do this without unduly limiting the functionality of your browser?

Answer: B. Disable the use of Third-party cookies.
Explanation: By disabling only Third-party cookies, web-site vendors will be able to use information from their own cookies but not those generated by another web-site.

25. How can a user lower the security requirements for Internet web-sites he trusts without changing these settings for other sites?

Answer: A. Change the Trusted Sites settings under Security in Internet Explorer Options.
Explanation: By configuring lower security requirements and specifying the specific sites under Trusted Sites other Internet web-sites will not be affected

26. You have been asked to enable the Content Advisor option in Internet Explorer on two users computers. They first of all want a

description of how it works. Which of the following statements is true of the Content Advisor configuration?

Answer: A. It affects all users who log into the machine.
Explanation: Content advisor is not profile specific. All users of Internet Explorer on that machine will be affected by the changes made.

27. You want to encrypt web traffic between your computer and the web-site of a vendor. How does your computer verify the Identity of the web server before doing this?

Answer: C. Certificates.
Explanation: Certificates issued by trusted third-party vendors can be used to verify the identity of the owner of a web-site

28. A user has disabled the use of all certificates on his computer. How will this affect his Internet browsing experience?

Answer: D. He will not be abe to connect to secure web-sites using HTTPS.
Explanation: Encrypted Internet connections that use HTTPS require the use of certificates

29. What feature of Internet Explorer allows you to fill out web forms without re-typing information that you have used on previous forms?

Answer: B. AutoComplete.
Explanation: AutoComplete uses the Profile Assistant to store user information sometimes used to fill out forms. This information can be used again in future forms without the need to re-type it.

30. A user asks for your help to configure Internet Explorer to save the password he uses for an Internet web-site. What can you tell the user?

Answer: D. This can be done using the AutoComplete option.
Explanation: AutoComplete can be configured to cache passwords for specific web-sites so they do not have to be re-entered.

31. Which of the following actions must be done before you can make a web-site available for offline access?

Answer: A. Add it to your Favorites.
Explanation: Before a web-site can be made available for offline access it must be added to the Favorites

32. Which of the following actions must you perform before deleting a synchronized web page?

Answer: D. Delete Temporary Inernet Files.
Explanation: When deleting Temporary Internet Files you can use the option to DELETE ALL OFFLINE CONTENT to accomplish this.

33. Which of the following configuration options is not available when setting up Outlook Express?

Answer: C. Connecting to Microsoft Exchange Server.
Explanation: Although there is no configuration option for directly connecting to an Exchange Server this can be done if the server is using other services such as IMAP. Outlook has configuration options for setting up links to Exchange Servers.

34. Which of the following features is available when configuring Outlook Express?
Answer: B. Contacts.
Explanation: Contacts are used to store e-mail addresses. The other features are only available on Outlook.

35. Outlook Express stores e-mails in files using what extension?

Answer: C. dbx.
Explanation: All Outlook Express files have a dbx extension e.g. inbox.dbx or drafts.dbx

36. Besides using Outlook Express what other way is there to create Identities?

Answer: A. Address Book.
Explanation: Identities can be created without using Outlook Express if you use the Address Book in Accessories. Creating multiple Identities makes it possible for users on the same machine to work with different configurations of Outlook Express.

37. You are looking for the Windows Address Book saved on a users flash drive. Which of the following files is most likely the one you are looking for?

Answer: A. data.wab.
Explanation: Windows Address Book files normally have an extension of wab.

38. Which of the following describes a service provided by Outlook Express but not available using Outlook?

Answer: C. Access to Newsgroups.
Explanation: Newsgroups can be accessed from Outlook Express but not from Outlook?

39. Which of the following is not a protocol used by Outlook Express to provide access to services?

Answer: B. SNTP.
Explanation: SNTP (Simple Network Time Protocol) is not used by Outlook Express.

40. Which of the following port numbers is used by Outlook Express to connect to a News Server?

Answer: A. 119.
Explanation: The NNTP protocol is used to connect to a news server and it uses port 119.

41. What tool would you use to configure multi-language support on your system?

Answer: B. Regional and Language Options.
Explanation: Language and Currency settings can be configured in the Control Panel using Regional and Language Options

42. You need to create a new hardware profile for your laptop to use it at home without its docking station. Which tool can you use to do this?

Answer: C. System Properties.
Explanation: System Properties has a Hardware folder where your hardware profile settings can be modified.

43. You want to install the latest updates to Microsoft Office Word 2003. What is the best way to get access to this information?

Answer: C. Use the Check for Updates option under Help in the Word application.
Explanation: Office products have their own links to the updates available on the Microsoft web-site

44. You want to configure the Microsoft Office Word 2003 application on your computer to create documents that are more compatible with Word 2000. What is one way that this can be done?

Answer: A. In Word 2003 use Tools > Options > Compatibility.

Explanation: By configuring the Compatibility options in the Tools menu of the application you can accomplish this task.

45. You need your Microsoft Office applications to save files you are working on automatically every 5 minutes. Which option must you configure to do this?

Answer: D. AutoRecover.
Explanation: The AutoRecover option allows you to specify that files you are working on must be automatically saved and the time interval for doing so.

46. You want Word 2003 to ignore capitalized words when it does a spell check on your documents. How should this be done?

Answer: B. On the menu bar go to Tools > Options > Spelling & Grammar.
Explanation: The spell check options can be modifed in Tools > Options > Spelling & Grammar

47. A user wants to disable the offline access of a web-site in Internet Explorer. How can this be done?

Answer: A. Change the properties of the web-site link in Favorites.
Explanation: Offline access for a web-site can be removed by disabling the Make Available Offline option in the properties of the link in your favorites

48. You want to clear the list of all web-sites you have previously visited from Internet Explorer. Which of the following options will do this?

Answer: C. Clear History.
Explanation: The History lists all web-sites you have previously visited in the last X number of days where X is configurable by you.

49. You want to configure Internet Explorer to automatically delete the list of names for web-sites you have browsed in the past. Only names that have been in the list for five days or more should be removed. How can you do this?

Answer: A. Modify the History settings in Tools > Internet Options > General.
Explanation: The number of days web-sites are kept in the History can be configured in Internet Options

50. A user is working on a computer where Internet Explorer is in Full-Screen mode and he is not able to access the menu options. How can he quickly reconfigure it so he can work with the menu options?

Answer: A. Press F11.
Explanation: The F11 function key will toggle between Full Screen and regular mode.

51. You need to import an Address book into Outlook Express. What extension will the address book file likely have?

Answer: B. wab.
Explanation: Address book files normally have an extension of wab

52. A user asks you to configure Outlook Express to use a second address book that holds personal information in addition to the one it is already using. How can you help this user?

Answer: D. Tell the user it cannot be done.
Explanation: Outlook Express can only use one address book.

53. You need to configure your browser to perform Integrated Windows Authentication. How can this be done?

Answer: A. Modify the Internet Options in Internet Explorer.

Explanation: Integrated Windows Authentication can be enabled by using the menu options in your Internet Explorer browser.

54. You need to limit the amount of space used on your hard-drive for Temporary Internet Files. Where can this be done?

Answer: B. In the Internet Options of Internet Explorer.
Explanation: The space used by Temporary Internet Files can be controlled from General folder of the Internet Options in Internet Explorer

55. A user wants to activate his copy of Office 2003 for his home computer but does not have an Internet connection. What is his next best option?

Answer: A. Activate it by telephone.
Explanation: Activation must be done via the Internet or Telephone otherwise the product will stop being functional.

56. You need to automate the installation of Office 2003 on the computers in your network. You have an Active Directory domain of which all the client computers are members and they all run Windows XP. Which of the following methods will accomplish the automated install?

Answer: C. Group Policy.
Explanation: Group Policy can be used in an Active Directory domain to install software on member computers.

57. A user on your network has gone on a three week business project which might turn into months. He calls to tell you that the copy of Office 2003 on his computer was not activated before he left on the trip. He periodically connects to the office through a VPN connection but you will not be able to work on his system until he comes back. What should you advise him to do?

Answer: B. Do the Activation himself over the Internet.
Explanation: He can activate the product himself by phone or over the Internet.

58. During the initial install of Office 2003 on your desktop you did not install Access. You have now changed your mind and need to install. How should this be done?

Answer: A. By customizing the Office install from Add/Remove Programs.
Explanation: You can simply modify the installation by changing the configuration of Office 2003 in Add/Remove programs. It will automatically look for the additional components in the initial install location.

59. A user mistakenly deletes some DLL files needed to run Office 2003 products. What is the easiest way to replace these files?

Answer: D. Repair Office 2003 from Add/Remove Programs.
Explanation: The repair process is the best way to replace deleted files.

60. You are working on an important document in Word 2003 when the application freezes and you are unable to save your changes. What is the best way to make sure that you recover as much of the document as possible?

Answer: A. Use the Microsoft Office Application Recovery tool.
Explanation: When the Microsoft Application Recovery tool is used to close an application it will attempt to save the file you are working on first.

61. A user has accidentally deleted an important department document from a network share and needs to restore the document as it existed the evening before. Which of the following methods will do this most efficiently?

Answer: C. Shadow Copy Restore.
Explanation: Shadow Copies save a file on a network share at specific times of the day when it is scheduled. The user is able to restore the file without administrator intervention.

62. A user has accidentally deleted a file from his local hard-drive and needs to restore it. Which of the following methods will do this most efficiently?

Answer: C. Tape Restore.
Explanation: Shadow Copies and Offline files only work for shared network resources and System Restore is used to fix O.S. problems

63. One of your users is unable to add a new word to his custom dictionary in Word 2003. What is one possible reason for this?

Answer: A. The dictionary has too many words.
Explanation: A custom dictionary can only hold 5000 words. Additional dictionaries can be created to add more recognized words to the system.

64. What feature of Office applications will automatically fix incorrectly typed words?

Answer: B. AutoCorrect.
Explanation: AutoCorrect will correct typos automatically without having to run a spell check.

65. A user is trying to modify the location and size of the toolbars in Internet Explorer but is unable. What is one possible reason for this?

Answer: D. The toolbars are locked.
Explanation: Locked toolbars cannot be moved. You can unlock a toolbar by right clicking on it and unchecking the Lock option.

66. Which of the following menu options will allow you to modify the toolbars used in a Microsoft Office 2003 product?

Answer: C. View > Toolbars.
Explanation: You can modify the toolbars being used by right clicking on them or using View > Toolbars in the menu options.

67. A user is searching for his personal folder file from Outlook using Windows Explorer. What file extension should he look for?

Answer: B. pst.
Explanation: Personal Folder files have a pst extension by default. They will only have an ost extension if they are Offline Folders.

68. You need to configure a users Outlook client on his laptop to use RPC over HTTP when accessing e-mail. Which of the following is required for this configuration to work?

Answer: D. Outlook 2003.
Explanation: The Outlook client must be version 2003 to configure RPC over HTTP.

69. You are helping a user who wants to access his corporate e-mail over the Internet using Outlook 2003. How can this be done without using a VPN connection?

Answer: C. Configure RPC over HTTP.
Explanation: RPC over HTTP allows you to use the HTTP protocol to access e-mail from an Exchange Server using your Outlook client. Both the client and server must be version 2003.

70. You need to fix an Outlook Personal Folder file for one of your users. Which of the following commands can you use to do this?

Answer: D. scanpst.

Explanation: scanpst.exe is used to fix Outlook Personal Folder files and Offline files.

71. A user is unable to access some of his e-mail messages from a computer he logs into. When he logs into his original computer all the messages are where they should be in Outlook. What could be causing this problem?

Answer: B. Some of his messages are stored in a Personal Folder file.
Explanation: If the messages are in a pst file on the local drive of the first computer he would not be able to access them on the second one.

72. You want to configure your Outlook client to automatically delete messages that are more than 30 days old. What feature will allow you to do this?

Answer: A. AutoArchive.
Explanation: AutoArchive allows you to delete and archive files on a schedule and also to specify different message criteria such as age.

73. You want to configure rules to manage your incoming e-mails more efficiently. Which of the following statements is not true of using rules in Outlook 2003?

Answer: B. They can support all client protoocol connection types.
Explanation: Rules are supported for all protocol connection types except HTTP

74. You are reconfiguring the e-mail profile of a user and need to locate their Personal Address Book on the computer. What file extension will this file have?

Answer: C. pab.
Explanation: Personal Address Books have a default extension of pab.

75. A user wants to be able to use his personal address book and the corporate one when he works in an Outlook profile. What can you tell him about this configuration?

Answer: D. He can import the address book and use it along side the existing corporate one.
Explanation: Outlook provides support for using multiple address books.

76. You want to configure RPC over HTTP in Outlook 2003 for e-mail access over the Internet. Which of the following requirements must be in place for this to work?

Answer: A. You must be running Windows XP with at least Service Pack 1 and appropriate hotfixes.
Explanation: Service Pack 1 and the Q331320 hotfix are needed for this to work

77. You need to configure an Outlook profile to cache e-mails on the client computer. The e-mail messages must not be removed from the server and you want automatic synchronization periodically. What option will allow you to configure these features?

Answer: B. Cached Exchange Mode.
Explanation: When using Cached Exchange Mode the information from the Exchange Server is cached on the local machine and changes are periodically synchronized with the server.

78. Which of the following name resolution methods uses a text file that has NETBIOS names to IP address mappings?
Answer: A. lmhosts.
Explanation: lmhosts is used for NETBIOS name resolution

79. Which of the following tools can you use to troubleshoot problems with DNS name resolution?

Answer: C. nslookup.
Explanation: nslookup is a command-line tool that can be used to test and troubleshoot name resolution on any DNS server.

80. Which of the following UNC paths will connect you to a share named DATA2 on a server named SQLTWO in a domain named ABCMAPS?

Answer: A. \\SQLTWO\DATA2.
Explanation: The unc path is always formatted using the syntax \\COMPUTERNAME\SHARENAME.

81. Your computer is having trouble resolving names and you want to verify the IP address of your DNS server. Which of the following commands can you use to do this?

Answer: A. ipconfig.
Explanation: ipconfig with the /all parameter can be used to verify the IP address of the DNS server you are using.

82. Your system is unable to resolve the IP of a web server on your network. You have verified that the DNS server has the correct information for this computer. Which of the following name resolution methods is likely causing this problem?

Answer: D. hosts.
Explanation: The hosts file information is cached on the computer and this information is checked before going to the DNS server. If found there the computer will not verify that data with the DNS server but just go ahead and use it.

83. Which of the following commands can you use to verify the MAC address of a Windows XP computer on another subnet in your network?

Answer: D. nbtstat.
Explanation: nbtstat can be used to get the MAC address of a remote system. Arp only works if you have previously communicated with the system and it resides on your subnet.

84. After running ipconfig on a computer it displays a subnet of 0.0.0.0. What might cause this problem?

Answer: B. Another computer has the same IP address.
Explanation: A subnet mask of 0.0.0.0 can indicate that there is another computer on the network that has an identical IP address.

85. Which of the following commands will force your computer to register its name on the DNS server?
Answer: C. ipconfig /registerdns.
Explanation: ipconfig will register the computer name on the DNS server if the /registerdns parameter is used.

86. Which of the following commands will force your computer to remove the IP address it received from a DHCP server?

Answer: D. ipconfig /release.
Explanation: ipconfig with the /release parameter will remove the DHCP assigned address

87. After checking the IP configuration on a computer you find that it has an address of 169.254.34.16. Which of the following might you assume from this information?
Answer: D. The DHCP server has no more available IP addresses.
Explanation: When a client is not able to get an IP address from a DHCP server it assign itself one using the APIPA system. These self assigned IPs are always in the format 169.254.x.x.

88. You have been asked to configure the default gateway on a

computer that has an IP address of 192.168.17.54 and a subnet mask of 255.255.255.0. Which of the following addresses could work as the default gateway?

Answer: B. 192.168.17.50.
Explanation: The default gateway (or router address) must belong to the same network address as that of the IP used by the computer. It must therefore be 192.168.17.X.

89. A user has a computer with two network cards one of which is permantently connected to the Internet. He wants to share this connection with three other machines on his network using ICS. Where should this be done?

Answer: A. On the NIC card not connected to the Internet.
Explanation: ICS should be configured on the network card connected to the Internal network. Not the one on the Internet.

90. You need to configure your firewall to allow the forwarding of e-mail messages using SMTP. What port number will you be openning up to do this?

Answer: C. 25.
Explanation: SMTP works on port 25 by default.

91. After configuring a VPN client you successfully connect to the VPN server. You are unable to connect to any resources on the network however. What could be the cause of this problem?

Answer: A. The DHCP Server is down.
Explanation: After connecting to a VPN Server the VPN client needs an IP address from the server itself or a DHCP server. If this cannot be done it will not be able to communicate properly with other systems on the network.

92. Your VPN Server requires clients to use a tunneling protocol that provides the highest level of encryption using IPSEC. Which of the following protocols meets these criteria?

Answer: C. L2TP.
Explanation: L2TP provides the highest level of encryption using IPSEC to protect transmitted data.

93. You need to configure your network firewall to allow traffic for the Remote Desktop application. What port number will you need to open?

Answer: B. 3389.
Explanation: Remote Desktop (and Remote Assistance) listen by default on port 3389.

94. While trying to print a document in Microsoft Word you get a message indication that you were unable to connect to it. The printer is connected via a USB hub that also connects the USB keyboard you are using. Which of the following is a possible reason for the printer problem?

Answer: B. The Printer is turned off.
Explanation: Since the keyboard is obviously working then nothing is wrong with the USB hub. The wrong driver being installed for the printer would not prevent a connection to it. So the printer is possibly turned off.

95. You connect a flash drive to a USB port on your computer but are unable to have the system recognize it. You have not changed the configuration of your computer and were able to get a USB keyboard to work on the same port yesterday. What is one possible reason for this issue?

Answer: A. The flash drive is damaged.
Explanation: The USB device is working properly so there could be a

problem with the flash drive. Sometimes removing the device and trying the connection again helps in these situations.

96. The local printer on your system is connected by means of a USB Hub which also connects the keyboard and two other devices to your computer. Sometimes you have trouble printing documents and believe its because of the overloaded Hub. Which of the following would be the best solution to this problem?

Answer: B. Connect the printer to the computer using its own USB port.
Explanation: If the printer had its own connection directly to the computer it should alleviate this problem.

97. Which of the following tools would work best for testing connectivity problems between your Outlook client and Exchange Server?

Answer: B. rpcping.
Explanation: RPC is the protocol used to communicate between Outlook and Exchange Server. The rpcping command can troubleshoot problems with protocol on your network.

98. Your manager has instructed you to create a share but to hide it so it is not browsable on the network. How can you do this?

Answer: D. Put a $ sign at the end of the share name.
Explanation: Shares can be hidden by putting a dollar ($) sign as the last character in the share name. Shares like this will not be browsable using network tools.

99. Your system is running an unauthorized program that replicates itself and tries to propogate through the network using your e-mail client. How is this type of attack often classified?

Answer: A. Virus.

Explanation: Viruses will often try to propogate themselves and slow down or disable resources on your computer. Some will also destroy files and create security problems.

100. You need to make the Microsoft Office applications more secure on your desktops. Which of the following configuration settings would give you the most concern?

Answer: D. Macros.
Explanation: The use of Macros can be just as damaging to a system as the attack from a virus. Improperly coded macros can destroy files and other resources.

101. A user is unable to access any of his encrypted files on the local hard-drive. Which of the following reasons is a possible cause for this?

Answer: B. His password has been reset.
Explanation: When a users password is reset the account no longer has access to encrypted files or e-mails. A recovery agent will need to decrypt the files for him.

102. A user wants to password protect a confidential Microsoft Word document that he is working on. What can you tell the user to help him protect the file?

Answer: C. Use Microsoft Word to modify the properties of the file.
Explanation: In Microsoft Word you can use the Tools > Options > Save parameters to assign a password.

103. A user working with Microsoft Word 2000 on his Windows XP desktop wants to be able to encrypt documents he is working with. The files must be accessible from other document editors such as Wordpad. What can you tell him about doing this?

Answer: A. He can do this as long as the file is saved on an NTFS drive.
Explanation: Support for encrypting files is provided by the NTFS files system and is transparent to any application you work with.

104. You need to find out who is modifying a confidential department file from a share on a domain server. You enable auditing on the server to accomplish this. Where can the log information generated by this audit be found?

Answer: C. In the Security Log.
Explanation: The log information will be stored in the Event Viewer in the Security Log.

105. A new user has just been added to a domain group to give him access to a network share. He is still unable to connect to the UNC path however. What should the user do to solve this problem?

Answer: B. Log off and logon again.
Explanation: He needs a new access token describing his new privileges. Logging on again will solve the problem.

106. You need to give a user access to a network printer using her domain account. The printer is connected to a domain server running Windows Server 2003. What tool can you use to do this?

Answer: D. Active Directory Users and Computers.
Explanation: Computer Management can be used for local accounts but Active Directory Users and Computers must be used for domain user accounts.

107. You need access to another users encrypted file. What must be done for you to be able to read this document?

Answer: D. The user must change the list of encryption users.

Explanation: Changing the NTFS permissions would not help in this situation. The user who encrypted the file must add you to the list of users who can use a certificate to decrypt it.

108. You are trying to connect to a share named DATA2 on SERVER1 which is a member server in the CLASSROOM5.COM domain. What UNC what would you use to connect to this share?

Answer: A. \\SERVER1\DATA2.
Explanation: The UNC path is always in the format \\COMPUTERNAME\SHARENAME.

109. Some confidential company information might have been compromised in an attack on a managers computer. There is a high probability that the system is virus infected. Which of the following tasks will you NOT do before an investigation is finished?

Answer: D. Format the hard-drive.
Explanation: The computer should be checked out by a security team before the hard-drive data is destroyed.

110. All the desktop computers in your network are members of a Windows 2000 domain and running Windows XP. One of your users is unable to encrypt files on his system. No other user has this problem. What is a probable reason for this users problem?

Answer: C. A Local Computer Policy applied on his system.
Explanation: Since only his machine is affected it is likely that the problem is caused by a Local Computer Policy setting.

111. Two conflicting Group Policies have been applied in Active Directory. One installs an accounting program and the other prevents its instalation. How will Active Directory resolve this conflict?

Answer: B. The last policy in the heirarchy will have its settings

applied.
Explanation: Active Directory policies are applied in the order Site > Domain > OU. When there is a conflict the last policy to be applied will have its settings configured.

112. You want to implement new security settings to force all Windows XP systems in your workgroup to use IPSec when communicating with each other. What is the best way to configure this?

Answer: C. Local Security Policy.
Explanation: Group Policy cannot be used in a Workgroup environment. Your next best option is to configure Local Security Policy settings.

113. You want to control access to a confidential department Word document. You need to give some managers the ability to modify it and all other users the ability to read it. The document is on a FAT32 partition. What is the best way to accomplish this?

Answer: A. Use the Microsoft Word application to assign a Read password and a separate Modify password.
Explanation: Since the partition is FAT32 you cannot assign permissions. Microsoft Word has the ability to assign Read and Modify passwords which will work on any partition type.

114. You need to reconfigure Internet access for users on your network to prevent everyone except users in the Legal department from using the NetMeeting application. Where is the best location to configure these settings?
Answer: B. Proxy Server.
Explanation: The Proxy Server can be configured to centrally control access to the Internet for all users.

115. You are troubleshooting a computer that is not able to

communicate with desktops on foreign subnets. You can communicate successfully with other computers on the local subnet. What network setting is most likely causing this problem?

Answer: D. Default Gateway.
Explanation: The Default Gateway or router address controls access to foreign networks or subnets.

116. You need to start keeping a log of how a color printer on your network is being used. What audit policy must you enable to do this?

Answer: C. Object Access.
Explanation: To audit the use of the printer you must enable the audit policy for Object Access and also configure the precise audit settings on the printer itself.

117. Some new security settings have been applied through Active Directory to your desktop and you want them to take effect immediately without rebooting the system. Which of the following tools will do this?

Answer: A. gpupdate.
Explanation: The gpupdate tool can update Active Directory policies on your system without a reboot.

118. You need to confirm how Active Directory policies are being applied to a computer to fix a recurring problem with it. What command-line tool will show you the policy settings on the machine in a single report?

Answer: B. gpresult.
Explanation: gpresult will show you a report of all the policy settings that apply to the computer

119. You want to create a batch file to be used as a logon script to

automate the encryption of a folder on everyones C: drive. What command line tool can you use in this batch file to do the encryption?

Answer: C. cipher.
Explanation: cipher.exe is the command-line utility used to encrypt and decrypt files and folders.

120. A user is trying to encrypt a file on his Windows XP computer that is a member of a Workgroup. What is one possible reason for his inability to encrypt the file?

Answer: A. The partition is FAT32.
Explanation: You can only encrypt files on NTFS partitions. You do not need ownership of a file to encrypt it.

Appendix C: Study Guide 70-271

Exam Preparation Guide for 70-271			
INSTALLING A WINDOWS DESKTOP OPERATING SYSTEM	S	W	P
Answer end-user questions related to attended installations			
Troubleshoot installations & configure device boot order			
Troubleshoot failed installations by using setup log files			
Perform post installation configuration e.g. service packs			
Answer end-user questions related to unattended installations			
Configure a PC to boot to a network device			
Perform an installation using unattended installation files			
Answer end-user questions related to upgrading from a previous version of Windows			
Verify hardware compatibility for upgrade			
Verify application compatibility for upgrade			
Migrate user state data from an existing PC to a new PC			
Install a second instance of an O.S. on a computer			
MANAGING AND TROUBLESHOOTING ACCESS TO RESOURCES			
Answer end-user questions related to managing access to foders			
Monitor, manage and troubleshoot NTFS file permissions			
Manage and troubleshoot simple file sharing			
Manage and troubleshoot file encryption			
Answer end-user questions related to troubleshooting access to folders			
Create shared folders			

Configure access to shared folders on NTFS partitions			
Troubleshoot and interpret Access Denied messages			
Answer end-user questions related to printing locally & over the network			
Configure and manage local & network printers			
Answer end-user questions related to configuring offline files			
Configure and troubleshoot offline files			
Configure and troubleshoot offline file synchronization			
CONFIGURING AND TROUBLESHOOTING HARDWARE DEVICES AND DRIVERS			
Answer end-user questions related to configuring hard disks and partitions			
Manage and troubleshoot disk partitioning			
Answer end-user questions related to optical drives (e.g. CD-ROMs)			
Configure and troubleshoot removable storage devices			
Answer end-user questions related to configuring desktop display settings			
Configure display devices and display settings			
Troubleshoot display device settings			
Answer end-user questions related to configuring ACPI settings			
Configure and troubleshoot operating system power settings			
Configure and troubleshoot system standby and hibernate settings			
Answer end-user questions related to configuring I/O devices			
Configure and troubleshoot device settings			
Configure and troubleshoot device drivers for I/O devices			

Configure and troubleshoot hardware profiles			
CONFIGURING AND TROUBLESHOOTING THE DESKTOP AND USER ENVIRONMENTS			
Answer end user questions related to configuring the desktop and user environment			
Configure and troubleshoot task and toolbar settings			
Configure and troubleshoot accessibility options			
Configure and troubleshoot pointing device settings			
Configure and troubleshoot fast-user switching			
Answer end-user questions related to regional settings			
Configure and troubleshoot regional settings			
Answer end-user questions related to language settings			
Configure and troubleshoot language settings			
Answer end-user questions related to security settings			
Identify end-user issues caused by local security policies			
Identify end-user issues caused by network security policies			
Answer end-user questions related to user accounts			
Configure and troubleshoot local user accounts			
Answer end-user questions related to local group accounts			
Configure and troubleshoot local group accounts			
Answer end-user questions related to system startup issues			
Troubleshoot system startup problems			
Answer end-user questions related to user logon issues			
Troubleshoot local user logon issues			

Troubleshoot domain user logon issues			
Answer end-user questions related to system performance			
Use Help and Support to view and troubleshoot system performance			
Use Task Manager to view and troubleshoot system performance			
Use the Performance tool to capture system performance information			
TROUBLESHOOTING NETWORK PROTOCOLS AND SERVICES			
Answer end-user questions related to configuring TCP/IP settings			
Configure and troubleshoot manual TCP/IP configuration			
Configure and troubleshoot automated TCP/IP address configuration			
Configure and troubleshoot ICF			
Configure and troubleshoot host name resolution issues on a client			
Configure and troubleshoot NETBIOS name resolution issues			
Configure and troubleshoot a remote dialup connection			
Configure and troubleshoot a remote connection across the Internet			
Configure and troubleshoot Internet Explorer connections properties			
Configure and troubleshoot Internet Explorer security properties			
Configure and troubleshoot Internet Explorer general properties			
Use Remote Desktop to configure and troubleshoot an end user's desktop			
Use Remote Assistance to configure and troubleshoot an end user's desktop			
S - Study W - Work On			

P - Proficient

Appendix D: Preparation Guide 70-27

Exam Preparation Guide for 70-272			
	S	W	P
CONFIGURING AND TROUBLESHOOTING APPLICATIONS			
Answer end-user questions related to configuring Office applications			
Set application compatibility settings			
Troubleshoot application installation problems			
Configure and troubleshoot e-mail account settings.			
Configure and troubleshoot Internet Explorer			
Answer end-user questions related to configuring Outlook Express			
Configure and troubleshoot newsreader account settings			
Answer end-user questions related to configuring the operating system			
Configure and troubleshoot file system access and file permission problems			
Configure access to applications on multi-user computers			
Configure and troubleshoot application access on a multiple user client PC			
RESOLVING ISSUES RELATED TO USABILITY			
Resolve Issues related to Office application support features			
Resolve issues related to Internet Explorer support features			
Resolve issues related to Outlook Express features			
Resolve issues related to operating system features			
RESOLVING ISSUES RELATED TO APPLICATION CUSTOMIZATION			
Answer end-user questions related to customizing Office applications			

Customize toolbars			
Configure proofing tools			
Manage Outlook data			
Personalize Office features			
Resolve issues related to customizing Internet Explorer			
Resolve issues related to customizing Outlook Express			
Resolve issues related to customizing the O.S. to support applications			
Answer end-user questions related to customizing the O.S. to support applications			
Customize the Start menu and taskbar			
Customize regional settings			
Customize fonts			
Customize folder settings			
CONFIGURING AND TROUBLESHOOTING CONNECTIVITY FOR APPLICATIONS			
Identify and troubleshoot name resolution problems			
Identify and troubleshoot network adapter configuration problems.			
Identify and troubleshoot LAN, Routing and Remote Access configuration problems			
Identify and troubleshoot network connectivity problems caused by firewall configuration			
Identify and troubleshoot problems with locally attached devices			
CONFIGURING APPLICATION SECURITY			
Answer end-user questions related to application security settings			
Troubleshoot access to local resources			
Troubleshoot access to network resources			
Troubleshoot insufficient user permissions and rights			

Appendix D: Preparation Guide 70-272

	S	W	P
Answer end-user questions related to security incidents			
Identify a virus attack			
Apply critical updates			
Manage application security settings			

S - Study

W - Work On

P - Proficient

www.ingramcontent.com/pod-product-compliance
Lightning Source LLC
Chambersburg PA
CBHW051246050326
40689CB00007B/1081